Fables and the Art of Leadership

Fables and the Art of Leadership

Applying the Wisdom of Mister Rogers to the Workplace

by Donna D. Mitroff and Ian I. Mitroff

FABLES AND THE ART OF LEADERSHIP
Copyright © Donna D. Mitroff, Ian I. Mitroff, and the Fred Rogers Company, 2012.

All rights reserved.

First published in 2012 by
PALGRAVE MACMILLAN®
in the United States—a division of St. Martin's Press LLC,
175 Fifth Avenue, New York, NY 10010.

Where this book is distributed in the UK, Europe and the rest of the World, this is by Palgrave Macmillan, a division of Macmillan Publishers Limited, registered in England, company number 785998, of Houndmills, Basingstoke, Hampshire RG21 6XS.

Palgrave Macmillan is the global academic imprint of the above companies and has companies and representatives throughout the world.

Palgrave® and Macmillan® are registered trademarks in the United States, the United Kingdom, Europe and other countries.

ISBN: 978–1–137–00308–9

Library of Congress Cataloging-in-Publication Data

Mitroff, Donna D.
  Fables and the art of leadership : applying the wisdom of Mister Rogers to the workplace / Donna Mitroff and Ian I. Mitroff.
    p. cm.
  ISBN 978–1–137–00308–9 (hardback)
  1. Leadership. 2. Values. 3. Rogers, Fred.
  I. Mitroff, Ian I. II. Title.
  HD57.7.M58 2012
  658.4′092—dc23   2012024487

A catalogue record of the book is available from the British Library.

Design by Integra Software Services

First edition: December 2012

10 9 8 7 6 5 4 3 2 1

Transferred to Digital Printing in 2013

This book is dedicated to the memory and life of Fred McFeely Rogers. He will always live in our hearts.

Contents

List of Figures and Tables	ix
Preface	xi
Acknowledgments	xv
Introduction	1

Part I   The Fables

1	Connect	19
2	Concern	23
3	Creativity	27
4	Communication	31
5	Consciousness	33
6	Courage	37
7	Community	39

Part II   Interpretations of the Fables

8	Planet Purple vs. Planet Prism	45
9	Good Friends	55
10	No Bare Hands in This Land	59
11	The Bass Violin Festival	63
12	The Reluctant Ring-Bearer	71
13	Once Upon Each Lovely Day	77
14	Daniel Tiger and the Snowstorm	83
15	Concluding Remarks on Leadership	87

Part III   Putting the Seven Cs to Work

16	Specialized Topics	95
17	Planet Purple vs. Planet Prism Revisited	131

18	Good Friends Revisited	137
19	No Bare Hands in This Land Revisited	143
20	The Bass Violin Festival Revisited	149
21	The Reluctant Ring-Bearer Revisited	155
22	Once Upon Each Lovely Day Revisited	157
23	Daniel Tiger and the Snowstorm Revisited	161
24	Leadership Revisited	163
25	Concluding Topics	167

Exercises	175
Additional Reading	183
About the Authors	185
Fred Rogers' Biography	189
Notes	193
Bibliography	197
Index	199

List of Figures and Tables

Figures

8.1	Change Management Versus Leadership	53
16.1	S Versus N, Sensing Versus Intuition	111
16.2	T Versus F, Thinking Versus Thinking	113
16.3	J Versus P, Judging Versus Perceiving	114
16.4	Four Combined Types	115
16.5	Relationships Between the Seven Cs and Special Topics	128

Table

25.1	Main Personality Features of the Main Characters	172

Preface

Fred Rogers is one of the great icons of American culture. The values and philosophy for which he is famous have stood the test of time. They continue to provide hope, wisdom, and inspiration for millions from childhood through adulthood. With this book the authors aspire to help today's leaders and prepare tomorrow's leaders in the creation of healthier workplaces. At the outset we wish to make it clear that we present *our* interpretation of the work of Fred Rogers. Our interpretations come from our deep respect for him, for his body of work, and from our careful study of that body of work. Nevertheless, the interpretations and the application of Fred's principles to the world of work are ours and ours alone.

Fables and the Art of Leadership: Bringing the Wisdom of Mister Rogers to the Workplace brings those same values and philosophy of Fred Rogers to the exact setting where it is needed most of all—to you in your workplace. This book is for today's managers and executives as well as for people from all walks of life who aspire to become and be better leaders.

Our research convinces us that Fred's influence not only is very much alive and well today but also had a multiplying effect through the continual impact of stars in the popular culture that were deeply affected by Fred when they were young. Pop singer Ricky Martin told Rosie O'Donnell on her talk show in June of 2000 that as the youngest member of an immigrant family, he learned to speak English from watching *Mister Rogers' Neighborhood*. In the recent Broadway show *Everyday Rapture,* Sherie Renee Scott sings the songs that Fred Rogers wrote and gives a "revelatory interpretation" of how Mister Rogers and his music helped steer her through the difficulties of adolescence.

And at age 4, Grammy Award-winning singer Esperanza Spalding reminisced that after watching classical cellist Yo-Yo Ma perform on an episode of *Mister Rogers' Neighborhood,* it was suddenly very clear to her that she wanted to do something musical. "It was definitely the thing that hipped me to the whole idea of music as a creative pursuit."

For over 40 years, Fred Rogers told stories that enlightened and reassured three generations of children, parents, and grandparents. Those who watched *Mister Rogers' Neighborhood* when they were young are today's students, practicing managers, and leaders. *Fables and the Art of Leadership* helps them reconnect with the wisdom of Fred Rogers so that they have the emotional skills and fortitude to confront the difficult problems they face in school, work, and life. Most of all, the book helps them to produce healthy workplaces that are the emotional backbone of the new economy.

This book uses seven of the many stories Fred told throughout his long career. These seven stories were carefully selected because they illustrate specific principles so beautifully. They are the very same stories that today's adults listened to with rapt attention when they were children. The stories are so rich that they have great meaning for both children and adults. They are so powerful that they can be used as business case studies. This is precisely how they are used in this book.

Mister Rogers' Neighborhood existed (and still does in reruns, on DVDs, and from free online sources) to help foster the emotional health and well-being of children. *Fables and the Art of Leadership* exists to help foster the emotional health and well-being of adults, especially in school, that is, colleges and universities, and at work, two of the settings where we spend the majority of our waking hours.

Fred's message is timeless and universal: to begin the process of making our workplaces healthy, we need to acknowledge that like neighborhoods, workplaces are made up of real, living, breathing people with diverse and complex needs.

We believe we need to acknowledge that while money is important, we do not work for money alone. Survey after survey show that in addition to money, we work primarily to find meaning and purpose in our lives. We want to be recognized for our contributions. We want to feel that through our work we are contributing to the well-being of others, that our organizations are ethical, and that both our organizations and we are serving authentic human needs. This, we believe, is the heart of Fred's message. It is also the heart of being a leader.

Fables and the Art of Leadership talks openly about feelings and also about the spiritual dimensions of being a leader. Both are conspicuously absent in the overwhelming majority of books and texts on management and leadership. *Fables and the Art of Leadership* is not an ordinary text. It does not propound abstract principles or feature long didactic discussions that are devoid of feeling, and which unfortunately constitute the majority of academic books on management and leadership. Instead, this book uses the heartrending fables and stories from *Mister Rogers' Neighborhood* to help readers appreciate the deep emotional and spiritual sides of leadership.

Acknowledgments

This book has been a labor of love for nearly ten years. While the words and interpretations are certainly ours, we never could have completed the project without the help and support of many people along the way. We offer our heartfelt thanks to those who have helped to make the book possible and our humble apologies to those helpers we have neglected to mention.

First and foremost, we thank our friends at the Fred Rogers Company. Bill Isler, chief executive officer at FRC, has stood by us through all of the ups and downs of the project. He encouraged us from the first glimmer of the idea through its final development. Bill championed the project and provided generous access to all of the materials in the Fred Rogers archives. Hedda Sharapan's deep and thorough knowledge of Fred's work along with her willingness to share it has been a gift of immeasurable benefit. We are indebted to her for helping us navigate Fred's many hours of programming to find the best fables to illustrate the points we wished to make. Cathy Droz read and provided helpful feedback on early drafts of the manuscript. Her input has made the book stronger. David Newell, also known as Mr. McFeely, not only let us know when references to Fred's work appeared in popular culture, but also provided constant support and encouragement from the beginning. Without the help and support from these good friends from the "Neighborhood," this book would not have been possible.

Joanne Byrd Rogers, Fred's wife, has become a dear and beloved friend over the years. Joanne gives her loving heart and keen intelligence to those efforts that enhance Fred's legacy. Donna has been especially privileged to work with Joanne on the Fred Rogers Memorial Scholarship, which is seeding the children's media industry with young people who will continue Fred's legacy of good work for children. We have been privileged to have Joanne's support for our book.

We owe a debt of gratitude and thanks to Professor Jyotzna Sanzgiri of Alliant International University. Jo read early drafts of the book and never waivered in her support over the years. She also allowed us to present the fables in one of her management classes. The feedback we gained from Jo and her students was invaluable.

Long-time friends and colleagues Warren Bennis, Ralph Kilmann, David Brancaccio, Joan Goldsmith, Kenneth Cloke, and Murat Alpaslan read and commented on several prior drafts. Their input and support has made the book better in more ways than we can say.

Susan McCombs has been our indefatigable book assistant. Not only has Susan handled the entire permissions process, prepared bibliography and references, and formatted the manuscript, but she also combed the entire manuscript for consistency and made valuable editorial suggestions.

We also cannot thank Joan Marques enough for steering us to Palgrave MacMillan. Through Joan's introduction we met our exceptional Palgrave team, Samantha Hasey and Leila Campoli. Thank you Sam and Leila for your encouragement, support, and help throughout every step of the process.

As Fred Rogers said, "All of us, at some time or other, need help. Whether we're giving or receiving help, each one of us has something valuable to bring to this world. That's one of the things that connects us as neighbors—in our own way, each one of us is a giver and a receiver."

> We have been blessed by the help of so many good neighbors along the way. Thank you.
> —Donna and Ian Mitroff

> If we can make every neighborhood like Mister Rogers' Neighborhood, America would be a happier place.
> —President Bill Clinton

> [Fred Rogers] is the only human being on TV to whom you would entrust the future of the world.
> —Gloria Steinem

Introduction

A Special Tribute to Fred Rogers

On December 9, 2003, we were privileged to participate in the special memorial "A Tribute to Fred Rogers," at the Academy of Television Arts and Sciences in North Hollywood, California. Over the course of the evening, members of the Hollywood elite paid their regards to a kind and gentle man who was the antithesis of what the entertainment industry generally represents. And yet, one after another, well-known personalities acknowledged Fred's illustrious career. Throughout the evening, Lily Tomlin, David Hartman, Tyne Daly, LeVar Burton, Scott Bakula, and many others sang, danced, and even cried as they recalled Fred's enormous contribution to children's television, the overwhelming influence that he had on their lives, their children, and even their grandchildren. All who attended spoke to Fred's authenticity and genuineness, and, especially, about how he gave everyone the hope that good television is possible.

Donna was one of the producers of the academy tribute. She met Fred in 1979, when she came to work at the Pittsburgh public television station, WQED, as Director of Educational Services. Fred's production company, Family Communications, Inc. (FCI), was and still is based at WQED. (FCI is now the Fred Rogers Company, or FRC.)

Donna worked with Fred and other members of his team over the next three decades and eventually came to know his wife, Joanne Byrd Rogers. While a member of the Board of Governors of the Academy of Television Arts and Sciences, Donna lobbied hard to get Fred elected to the Academy's Hall of Fame. In July of 2002, Fred was inducted into the academy.

During the months that it took to develop "A Tribute to Fred Rogers," Donna reviewed and reread most of Fred's writings. As she rediscovered the depth and breadth of Fred's ideas and shared these discoveries with Ian, a fundamental realization took shape: what Fred wrote and said about human development applies equally to adults as it does to children.

This led to many hours of conversation and reexaminations of Fred's writings to see if our initial suspicion held up. It did. In fact, Ian pointed out that the process of translating the principles of Fred Rogers from helping children grow and develop into healthy adults resulted in concepts that were far more profound than what is generally expounded in management education and leadership.

Seven Key Principles: The Seven Cs

Through the many hours we have spent analyzing and pondering Fred's work, we derived seven key principles—The Seven Cs—that apply not only to work but also to the essence of being a leader. They apply equally to life in general. Each is illustrated through a direct quote from Fred:

1. *Connect*: "A person can grow to his or her fullest capacity only in mutually caring relationships with others."
2. *Concern*: "Setting rules is one of the primary ways in which we show our love."
3. *Creativity*: "Play is the expression of our creativity, and creativity, I believe, is at the very root of our ability to learn, to cope, and to become whatever we may be."
4. *Communication*: "In times of stress, the best thing we can do for each other is to listen with our ears and our hearts and to be assured that our questions are just as important as our answers."
5. *Consciousness*: "Take good care of that part of you where your best dreams come from, that invisible part of you that allows you to look upon yourself and your neighbor with delight."
6. *Courage*: "One of the greatest paradoxes about omnipotence is that we need to feel it early in life, and lose it early in life, in order to achieve a healthy, realistic, yet exciting sense of potency later on."

7. *Community*: "All of us, at some time or other, need help. Whether we're giving or receiving help, each one of us has something valuable to bring to this world. That's one of the things that connects us as neighbors—in our own way, each one of us is a giver and a receiver."

The order of the principles is important. They proceed from the most basic and concrete to the more complex so that by the last chapter, students and managers alike are better able to face and confront the enormous changes and challenges facing today's organizations.

Each principle is illustrated in this book through a combination of carefully selected fables and quotes from Fred's life and writings. Most important of all, we have provided carefully selected questions at the end of each fable to help readers discover for themselves what the principles mean to them and how they apply to their lives and organizations. Whether one is working or not, everyone comes in contact with organizations daily. The fables are applicable to everyone.

The seven principles are the key to making healthy and productive workplaces that can compete successfully in the global economy. Our argument is that without practicing and deeply embodying the principles, leaders will not grow and develop, and organizations, as we know them, will not survive.

The Centerpiece

Fred's original fables are the centerpiece of *Fables and the Art of Leadership*. The selected fables are brief retellings of stories that were portrayed in episodes of *Mister Rogers' Neighborhood*.

Fred did not expound abstract principles for the children, parents, and grandparents who watched *Mister Rogers' Neighborhood*. Instead, he told countless stories and created fables to forge deep and personal connections with each of his viewers.

Stories and fables engage and hold the attention of young children. They are also one of the main ways in which one gains the attention of adults. But they are even more basic. Humans are the only creatures that invent and listen to fables and stories. They are the essence of what make us human.

Through the use of fanciful characters, animals, and magic, fables take us out of everyday reality, transport us to places and situations that are sharper and larger than life, and thereby teach us profound moral lessons. Fables impact us as few forms of communication do because hit us squarely in our guts and in our souls. Because they apply to every aspect of life, every one of them has fundamental lessons for leadership.

"The Bass Violin Festival" (Chapter 3) is one of the many stories from the "Neighborhood of Make-Believe" (NMB), the magical place that Fred took viewers to visit during every show. The purpose of the fable is to help readers understand better the nature and the process of creativity. As Fred put it, "Play is the expression of our creativity, and creativity I believe, is at the very root of our ability to learn, to cope and to become whatever we may be."

In our interpretation of the fable as a "mini-business case," King Friday (the stand-in for today's CEOs) tells all his subjects (employees) that they must be prepared to play the bass violin (a skill at which he is an expert) at an upcoming festival (corporate meeting). Only when the subjects take the time to play creatively—that is, figuratively, and not literally, play the violin—do they come up with solutions that enable them to conquer their fears of not having the technical expertise (job skills) to complete the assignment (job). Only in this way, can they then contribute to the festival (meeting) by using their individual, unique talents. The principles and lessons embedded in the story show how everyone can step back from a difficult assignment, reframe it, and produce creative solutions.

This is precisely what we need to do if we are to overcome the countless fears associated with the difficult and rocky transformation to the new global economy. The new economy requires people who can think creatively and, hence, exercise critical thinking. While many aspects of blue-collar and even white-collar jobs are already completely automated, creativity and critical thinking will never be. As a result, these skills can never be outsourced. They are the only true and lasting competitive edge.

Fred's Influence

A letter that Family Communications Inc., Fred's TV production company in Pittsburgh, received some years ago is a perfect example of how strong Fred's influence was on adults as well as on children. A young man wrote to tell Mister Rogers how he had come to the end of his first semester at college and was horrified when his grades came back so much lower than he had expected and were needed to get into medical school. He remembered thinking "I'm really going down the drain!" When he came back to his dorm and turned on the TV in search of distraction, there was Mister Rogers singing "You Can Never Go Down the Drain," one of Fred's many songs designed to deal with the inner life of children, that is, the countless fears as well as joys that all young children have. The young man remembered how he stopped, listened carefully to the song, and understood at a deep level that he *could not* "go down the drain." Then and there, he resolved that he "*would not* go down the drain." He wrote how he buckled down and went on to successfully complete medical school.

The significance of this story is that even as a young adult, the young man benefited from Mister Rogers. We don't know if this particular young man had viewed *Mister Rogers' Neighborhood* as a child but chances are that he did. The point is that at a time that was especially trying in his life, he was able to turn to Fred Rogers and find the support he needed. The song that Fred Rogers was singing, "You Can Never Go Down the Drain," is one that Fred describes as "responsive to a widely shared 'inner drama' of early childhood."

In early childhood, the child's inner drama is perceived and experienced as real and literal. Young children actually worry that they could be literally sucked down the drain along with the drain water. When we reach adulthood, the inner drama is figurative or metaphorical, as it was in the case of the young college student. Nevertheless, the root of the fear, or inner drama, is lodged in deep, unremembered fears from childhood. That is why Fred Rogers continues to speak to us from childhood through adulthood. His messages are so finely honed to the inner dramas of our lives that we can continue to respond at different levels of our development and stages of our lives.

Another example of Fred Rogers' continuing influence on adults occurred soon after his death in 2003. *Pittsburgh Magazine* devoted the April 2003 issue entirely to Fred's legacy. Betsy Benson's "Publisher's Note" in that issue is a vivid testimony to Fred's long-lasting impact:

> During his lifetime, Fred Rogers did a remarkable thing: He created a brand-new language, comprising thousands of simple words and images that speak of truth, love, respect and caring. He hoped that adults and children would learn his language and apply it in their daily lives. Based on the more than 600 e-mail messages that flooded our website following his death on Feb. 27, many did indeed learn that language. In fact, one of the recurring themes in the e-mails is the value that adults continue to place on Fred Rogers' words. Unabashedly, they talk of tuning into *Mister Rogers' Neighborhood* after losing a job or when facing a personal crisis. They speak tenderly of the life lessons they learned during Fred's "television visits".

Over the course of 40 continuous years on television, Fred Rogers has had an enormous influence on adults who are the current leaders, managers, and employees and decision makers of society. It is doubtful that many leaders are aware of this influence. But we know one who is and her statement about Fred's influence is profound.

Anne Sweeney co-chair, Disney Media Networks, and president, Disney-ABC Television Group, was also one of the people who spoke about Fred Rogers in December 2003, at the special "A Tribute to Fred Rogers." Ms. Sweeney spoke directly about Fred Rogers' influence on her management style:

Fred not only influenced me as he did thousands of others when I was a kid, but he continues to influence me even more as an adult. The most important lesson I learned from Fred was the importance of listening with one's entire being. From him, I learned how to be fully and completely in the moment with whomever I was engaged. I learned how to listen to the inner person. That is the essence of being a true leader.

Two Basic Questions

Fred's countless influence on adults leads us to ask two basic questions: First, how is it possible that a television personality known primarily for his kind and simple method of communicating with young children can also be a source of workplace wisdom for adults? Second, how can we tap that wisdom to help us both understand and deal with our individual issues at work and also improve our workplaces?

The answer to the first question is that Fred Rogers was no ordinary television personality. In addition to writing scripts, composing and performing music, and doing the puppeteering on the show, he wrote books, gave speeches, and appeared frequently at public gatherings. (See "Biography of Fred Rogers" at the back of this book.) Fred Rogers was a multitalented person.

But he went beyond these talents. During the early years of developing and producing *Mister Rogers' Neighborhood*, Fred undertook two important courses of study. One was to become a Presbyterian minister. The other was to study child development under some of the nation's leading child psychologists and child psychiatrists so that he could attain a deep understanding of the emotional needs of children.

Fred realized that his unique calling was to work with children and families through the mass media by focusing on television's "great potential for good." Children's television became his ministry.

As one examines Fred's work, one quickly sees that his understanding of emotional needs went far beyond child development into the larger realm of human development and that his ministerial work went beyond the realm of Presbyterianism into the realm of human purpose and spirituality. This is why Fred Rogers is a sage for our times. His life, his work, and his study, all prepared him to help humankind throughout all the stages of life.

The answer to the second question, "How can we tap that wisdom to help us both understand and deal with our individual issues at work and also improve our workplaces?," lies in the realm of storytelling to which we referred earlier. There is an old Hasidic proverb that says if you give a person a fact or an idea, you enlighten his or her mind, but if you tell a person a story, then you touch that person's soul. Storytelling both instructs and feeds the soul and spirit.

We cannot stress enough that throughout the 40 years of creating programs for *Mister Rogers' Neighborhood*, Fred and his team told hundreds of stories. Many of the stories dealt with the issues of everyday life—how things work, how people make the things we use, where things come from, and so on. But, as we noted earlier, many of the stories occurred in the NMB. The stories are so beautifully crafted that they speak to the basic inner dramas of human existence in ways that transcend the age of the listener. This is why Fred's wisdom resonates from childhood to adulthood. The stories in the NMB can be read and reread by children and grown-ups alike. Whatever our age, the stories speak to our hearts, our souls, and our spirits. They have lessons to teach us over the course of our lives.

The stories from *Mister Rogers' Neighborhood* and the NMB function in the same way that myths and fairytales have for centuries. They deal with universal human fears, needs, hopes, dreams, and lessons. Like myths and fairytales, many of the truths are revealed through symbols and metaphors that have one level of meaning for children and an entirely different one for adults.

A Brief Refresher about the NMB

A neighborhood is a place where diverse groups of people live not only in close physical proximity to one another, but more importantly, in close emotional proximity. A neighborhood becomes a community when its inhabitants both know one another and also give one another personal space and respect their privacy. But more importantly, a neighborhood becomes a community when people cooperate for the good of everyone and when they accept responsibility for their roles and tasks in support of the neighborhood.

Anyone who has ever watched *Mister Rogers' Neighborhood* knows that King Friday XIII is one of the major puppet characters. As he is described in the Fred Rogers Company website, what makes King Friday interesting is that just "beneath his pompous exterior, he is a lonely ruler who continually uses his power to make himself feel important. Inside, King Friday is a sympathetic soul who mellows when loved and appreciated." As we shall see, King Friday is a stand-in for many of today's CEOs.

Like King Friday, all of the characters on *Mister Rogers' Neighborhood* are complex creatures. In this way, they are like real people. Although they have been intentionally constructed to represent extremes so that young people will have little difficulty in recognizing their dominant personalities, they are not one-dimensional cardboard cutouts. Indeed, this is one of the central themes of Part III of this book.

The website for *Mister Rogers' Neighborhood* says it best:

> The stories [and the characters] in the Neighborhood of Make-Believe portray [the] common concerns of young children and a range of feelings that young children experience—anger, fear, envy, joy and pride. They illustrate how people [as members of caring neighborhoods] can work together and support each other, sharing their feelings with one another and modeling prosocial behavior. While the characters have identifiable personality characteristics, at the same time, they have the capacity for growing.

The complete set of characters that make up NMB is a mixture of puppets and live performers. Together they represent two things: one, the diversity that is *internal*—within each of us—and two, the diversity that is present in the larger human community *external* to us.

Real neighborhoods are made up of diverse types of people: young and old, well-off and not-so-well-off, well-educated and not-so-well educated, professional people and tradesmen, native born citizens and recent immigrants. Just as in a real neighborhood, the characters experience conflicts, get angry at one another, cry, scream, and laugh. In doing so, they learn that emotions and feelings are natural and that they can be handled in positive and constructive ways. They help one another because they care deeply about one another.

In addition to diversity, the characters represent something even more important. Each one represents a different aspect or component of emotional health, that is, what it means to be a healthy person. That's why they have such a deep appeal. If we can learn from each of them and try to integrate each of their best sides within us, then every one of us can be, in the words of Fred, "the best person we can be."

Let's take a brief look at some of the major characters in the neighborhood and the qualities for which they stand. We will refer to them throughout this book.

King Friday, a Puppet

We've already said a good bit about King Friday XIII (King Friday the 13th), but because he plays a central role in all the fables, we need to say more.

King Friday is the imperious monarch of the neighborhood. He is egocentric, irrational, resistant to change, and temperamental, although open-minded enough to listen when told he is wrong. He has a fondness for giving long-winded speeches and using big words. He is also easily distracted. For example, in one story, while his civil engineers were concerned about a water shortage in the kingdom, King Friday talked about building a swimming pool. Despite these qualities, he's basically a good ruler, capable of summarizing the lesson he has learned after something has gone wrong.

Queen Sara Saturday, a Puppet

Queen Sara Saturday is benevolent and diplomatic. She works on international task forces like the "Food for the World" committee. She is a nurturing mother to their son, Prince Tuesday, and a loving wife who understands the king and often mediates between him and his subjects.

Queen Sara stands for the benevolent soul, and that part of us that has deep concern for those less fortunate than us.

Lady Elaine Fairchilde, a Puppet

Lady Elaine is the curator of the Museum-Go-Round, a revolving building containing collections of everything from A to Z. This mischief-making impish woman is always getting into one situation or another, but that's often because she worries that she's not very lovable and needs attention. As an outspoken, opinionated character, she is generally the only one in the NMB who stands up to the king whenever he has made an unreasonable demand. And she often brings a lot of humor to the NMB.

Lady Elaine represents both the person who stands up to authority and the rebelliousness that is part of every child and the child that still lives in each of us.

Daniel the Stripèd Tiger, a Puppet

Daniel the Stripèd Tiger (also referred to as Daniel or Daniel Tiger in this book) is a shy, tame tiger who lives in a (nonfunctioning) grandfather clock with no hands because in make-believe it is whatever time you imagine. Despite his shyness, Daniel exhibits remarkable wisdom and intelligence when he manages to speak (he discerns the root of Lady Elaine's bad behavior on several occasions). He is the only child among the puppets whose parents are never seen, nor spoken of. He has a close friendship with Lady Aberlin, who often nuzzles his nose and says, "Ugga Mugga." His favorite toy is a small dump truck, and he wears a watch on one arm because, he explains, "when you live in a clock you really should know what time it is." Daniel mentions that he doesn't have grandparents, but would like some, and consequently gets some pretended ones. In July 2011, PBS announced that Daniel's son (also named Daniel) would be the star of his own show, *Daniel Tiger's Neighborhood*.

Lady Aberlin, a Live Performer

Lady Aberlin, niece of King Friday XIII, is a caring friend to the puppet characters and neighbors in the NMB. She is sensitive to the needs and feelings of her friends and knows how helpful it is to talk about things when the puppet characters are upset or concerned. She also enjoys celebrating with them when they're happy and proud. Lady Aberlin loves to dance.

Mr. Aber, a Live Performer

Charles R. Aber is the Westwood Neighbor. As the associate mayor of Westwood, he assists Mayor Maggie and is a kind neighbor to everyone in the NMB. As a good friend in the "real" neighborhood, he shares his many interests with Mister Rogers and his television friends.

Mr. McFeely, a Live Performer

Mr. McFeely, a grandfatherly character, runs the "Speedy Delivery Service" for the entire neighborhood. He sometimes delivers letters and packages to the citizens of the NMB. He is, along with Mr. Aber, one of the few characters to pass between Mr. Rogers' "real" world and the NMB.

Handyman Negri, a Live Performer

Handyman Negri is the friendly, avuncular neighborhood fix-it man. He is an accomplished guitarist, but in Make-Believe, he is the royal handyman, available to help with repairs around the kingdom. As a friend for the puppet characters and other neighbors, he's always there to lend a caring ear, a helping hand, and sometimes a song on his guitar.

Betty Templeton-Jones and James Michael Jones, Live Performers

Betty Templeton-Jones is a former schoolmate of Lady Elaine Fairchilde who now and then comes to visit in the Neighborhood of Make-Believe from nearby Southwood. She's a nonstop talker and always has something to say. Because she understands Lady Elaine so well, she is sometimes called on to help Lady Elaine out of a jam. James Michael Jones is also from the neighborhood of Southwood. He and Betty married in the Neighborhood of Make-Believe.

Bob Dog, a Costumed Performer

Bob Dog is a friendly playful canine. It is enthusiastic about lots of things, a trait that sometimes gets him into trouble.

Miss Paulifficate, a Costumed Performer

Miss Paulifficate is the telephone operator at the Castle. Storylines often allude to her former career as a dancer, and she often demonstrates her tap dancing abilities. She frequently takes the brunt of King Friday's bad moods.

Purple Panda, a Costumed Performer

Purple Panda is a two-toned purple panda from Planet Purple. He has a robotic, monotone voice. He arrives in the neighborhood by teleporting, which is "The Purple Way to travel."

Why This Book Is Especially Needed at This Time

There's never been a time in our history when there have been so many changes, so many unusual things to deal with and for which we have no experience. It's as if our whole society were walking along a road through a wilderness of constant change with strangers we think we should know, but don't quite understand.

—Fred Rogers

Fred's work is more relevant than ever. His ability to provide wise counsel that cuts directly to our deep needs couldn't be needed more than it is at present.

The unparalleled wave of recent corporate and institutional scandals, the decline in personal responsibility and ethics, the rise of rudeness and incivility, all of these and more call into question not only the ways that we have designed, managed, and operated organizations, but all the aspects of our lives.

According to the Conference Board, only 50 percent of Americans are happy with their jobs. Even more disturbing is the fact that this is down dramatically from 59 percent in 1995. At the same time, a recent survey appearing in the *Chicago Sun Times* (April 10, 2005) found that business and labor leaders are alarmed because they find that employees lack the basic abilities, and the willingness, to accept supervision and personal responsibility, to work well with diverse types of people, to participate in well-integrated teams, and to resolve conflicts and express feelings and thoughts in appropriate ways.

Few would deny that these and other basic skills and attitudes should have been learned in childhood. At the same time, management also should have learned by now that their organizations cannot compete in the world economy when only half of their employees find satisfaction in their jobs. Employees cannot be treated as though they do not have deep needs and feelings. People are not interchangeable, mechanical robots, or parts that can be discarded at will.

In the past four decades, the nature of work and organizations has changed dramatically. Once, a secure job for life with a single organization was the expectation in most Western cultures. One wouldn't necessarily get rich, but was assured of being able to provide for oneself and one's family and have a decent retirement to boot. Entire communities benefited from having stable and secure breadwinners.

Now one is lucky to have a good job at all. And there are few, if any, jobs for life.

But something even deeper has also been lost. It used to mean that joining an organization meant joining a special family for life. The key word is *family*. One was encouraged to feel as a member of something good and important, not just as an employee. Now, one's current resume and skill set are the key words in the workplace. The family has been replaced by a cold and impersonal system of virtual organizations in cyberspace.

Clearly, something is missing.

We believe that unless organizations are reconceptualized—reborn, as it were, as neighborhoods—we will not be able to compete successfully in the new global economy. To compete successfully, high levels of technical *and* personal competency are needed. Nonetheless, all the technical skills in the world cannot make up for not treating people with care, dignity, and respect.

A few organizations not only "get it" but also serve as role models for those organizations that have not yet figured it out. One example of an organization that "gets it" is Southwest Airlines. The company follows the direct and simple philosophy of *hire for attitude; train for skills*. In other words, while people and technical skills are equally important, we need to put greater emphasis on putting people first.

To begin the process of re-humanizing our workplaces, we need to acknowledge that workplaces, like neighborhoods, are made up of real, living, breathing people with diverse and complex needs. A central premise of *Fables and the Art of Leadership* is that a set of core principles—the Seven Cs—underlie Fred's work and that if these principles are successfully applied to workplaces, then we can turn our workplaces into neighborhoods. This is one of Fred Rogers' greatest legacies.

Three Equal Parts

The reader is urged to note that the book is divided into three equal and important parts. In Part I, we present Fred's fables with very little comment so that the reader is free to react to them and to form his or her own interpretations. In Part II, we offer our interpretations and extended commentary of the fables, and draw connections between

Fred's fables and the workplace. We also give our interpretations so that the reader can compare and contrast his or her understandings with ours. In Part III, we expand on the Seven Cs to show how they bear on some of the classic issues in organizational behavior. Indeed, they lead to some very different interpretations of familiar and not-so-familiar topics.

PART I

The Fables

Readers Guide: How to Read the Fables

Before you read the fables, let us reiterate briefly why they are important.

Fables, myths, and stories reach back to the very dawn of civilization itself. Long before humans learned to write and recorded their versions of history, they told stories to make sense of the seasons, marriage, birth, death, and any one of a thousand incidents and events.

Everyone is familiar with fables of one kind or another. Nearly everyone has heard of one or more of Aesop's Fables. The fable of "The Tortoise and the Hare" is so familiar that it's a part of our everyday vocabulary. It is so popular that there are cartoon versions of it for young children. Similarly, the fairy tales of Hans Christian Andersen are also part of our general makeup, so much so that we take them for granted. The Grimms Fairy Tales are equally familiar. And, of course, every culture has its own special myths and stories.

In spite of the immense variation among them, fables, myths, and stories share a number of common features. One, they generally take place in magical realms that are deliberately far removed from the constraints of the ordinary world. As a result, the characters can say and do things that they would never do in everyday life. In this way, they teach us lessons unencumbered by everyday reality. Two, they employ animal, mythic, and superhuman characters. The characters are deliberate, larger-than-life exaggerations of human qualities such that we can easily see both their good and bad sides, often simultaneously. Three, unlike in real life, things generally get resolved in happy, clear-cut endings. The "good guys" are rewarded and the "bad guys" are punished. And typically, there is a clear distinction between the good guys and the bad guys. Four, the resolutions generally come in the form of clear moral lessons or principles. There is little, if any, ambiguity to what we are supposed to learn.

Whether you've ever heard or read the fables included in this book before, pay careful attention to the feelings that each of the characters and the stories raise in you now. Do you instinctively like or dislike any of the characters or situations? Why? What aspects of the fables remind you of the organizations with which you are familiar, work for, and come in frequent contact with, and why? Do the characters do a better or worse job of solving problems than either you or the organizations do?

We cannot emphasize enough that Fred Rogers explicitly created all of the different characters that appear in his fables because he knew that each of them was an important, vital part of his own personality, and a part of everyone as well. Fred put it as follows:

> There's the good guy and the bad guy in all of us, but knowing that doesn't ever need to overwhelm us.

When we react strongly to a particular character, it is often because we like or don't like a particular part of ourselves. Or, perhaps, it is because the character reminds us of someone in our past that treated us either poorly or well.

CHAPTER 1

Connect

A person can grow to his or her fullest capacity only in mutually caring relationships with others.
—Fred Rogers

Good Friends

Everyone in the Neighborhood of Make-Believe is excitedly preparing for King Friday's upcoming picnic. Lady Aberlin is hurrying about preparing her contribution and listing all the things she still needs to do. Daniel Tiger slows her down long enough to say, in his shy way, that he would like to go to the picnic with her. She agrees to come by to pick him up after she finishes her errands.

Daniel keeps himself busy while he waits for Lady Aberlin to come back for him. Several neighbors pass by on the way to the picnic. When they ask him why he isn't coming to the picnic, he explains that he is waiting for a friend. Time passes and the trickle of passers-by slows down. Daniel thinks it must surely be time to go, so he puts his things away in readiness. Then he waits and he waits and he waits. It has become very quiet in the Neighborhood. Daniel is getting worried.

When Mr. McFeely stops by and asks why Daniel hasn't left for the picnic, Daniel explains that he is still waiting for Lady Aberlin. Mr. McFeely invites Daniel to come along with him.

Poor Daniel is concerned that if he goes with Mr. McFeely, Lady Aberlin might come by and be worried when he is gone, and yet, down deep he is afraid that she has forgotten him.

Mr. McFeely calls the castle to find out if Lady Aberlin is there. Indeed, she is, and when Mr. McFeely reminds her about Daniel, she feels terrible and says she will come straight back to Daniel's house. Soon, she rushes in saying, "I'm really sorry, Daniel." "Are you? Are you really?" Daniel asks her sadly. Lady Aberlin acknowledges to Daniel that she did indeed forget her promise to pick him up. She also acknowledges that she knows that it feels awful to be forgotten. Daniel wants to know why she forgot him. Well, her only explanation is that she was hurrying around, getting her errands done, and it slipped her mind.

"Has being forgotten ever happened to you?" Daniel asks. Lady Aberlin stops to think and remembers that, yes, once when she was a little girl and it was her birthday, her best friend forgot to come to the party. "Were you mad at your friend for forgetting?" Daniel asks. Lady Aberlin explains that she was not actually mad, that what she felt was deep disappointment. "Did your friend forget you because she was mad at you?" Daniel asks. "No," Lady Aberlin says, "My friend didn't miss the party because she was mad. She just forgot."

Daniel presses for an explanation. "But, why did you forget me?" he asks again.

"Does it make you feel like we're not really friends when you hear that I just forgot to come and pick you up?" she asks.

"Yes," Daniel blurts out, "I feel that we are not really friends if you can just forget about me."

When Lady Aberlin starts to apologize again, Daniel stops her saying that he feels better because they had a good talk. "I'm ready to go to the castle now." Daniel says. "I'm ready too," says Lady Aberlin.

The picnic is a wonderful time. When King Friday invites each person to put his or her own words to music, Queen Sara Saturday sings the following song:

> There are many ways to say I love you
> There are many ways to say I care about you
> Many ways, many ways, many ways to say I love you...

Each neighbor takes a turn singing about the different ways to say "I love you." There is the sharing way; there is the "letting someone play with something that you like" way; there is the listening way. When it is Daniel's turn, he sings about how important it is to take time to really understand how another person feels. Daniel says that is an important way to say "I love you."

It's important to pay special attention to your feelings as you read a fable. Indeed, how you feel when reading fables is the whole point of reading and sharing them. You are the primary judge with regard to what it raises in you, and how you feel about the characters and the story itself.

- Consider these ideas: One of the primary themes in the fable is the feeling of being abandoned that all of us have at one time or another. Another is the feeling of being let down by friends, left behind, or left out. But what else does it strike you that the fable is about? And how does it apply to those organizations in which you've ever worked or with which you've had contact? How does it apply to your life? How does it apply to being in school?
- What does the fable say about being able to name feelings, and to name them accurately? As Fred said, "Whatever is human is mentionable. Whatever is mentionable is manageable." How does this statement apply to the feelings that Daniel had? How does this statement apply to a miscommunication you might have had with a member of an organization or a member of your family? Again, how does it apply to school?

Hold onto your impressions of and feelings about the characters in "Good Friends" and see if they change as you go through the other fables.

CHAPTER 2

Concern

Setting rules is one of the primary ways in which we show our love.
—Fred Rogers

No Bare Hands in This Land

One bright, lovely day, King Friday announces to Handyman Negri that he has made a new rule for the day: that there are to be no bare hands in the land; everyone is to wear mittens. Handyman Negri comments that he has many jobs to do and that it will not be easy to work while wearing mittens. King Friday responds that he never promised him an "easy job" and, further, that he expects Handyman Negri to go around the kingdom and alert everyone about the new rule.

Each person he tells wants to know why he or she must wear mittens. No one knows the reason, but they all assume that King Friday "must have a good reason." They also note that they will not be able to complete their current tasks while wearing mittens. Nevertheless, they stop what they are doing and put on their mittens. That is, everyone except Lady Elaine Fairchilde does. When she learns about the new rule, she insists on knowing why. Handyman Negri admits that he didn't ask the king why; he only knows that the rule applies to everybody. Lady Elaine responds, "Well, here's one body that isn't everybody and I won't do it unless I know the reason." She proclaims that she is going straight to the castle to ask King Friday for an explanation.

As soon as King Friday sees Lady Elaine, he reminds her of the new rule and asks, "Where are *your* mittens?" Lady Elaine defiantly replies, "They are home in my drawer and they will stay there until you tell me why you have made this rule."

"In 17½ seconds, you will know the reason," says King Friday. Soon others, all wearing their mittens, gather at the castle. While they are still curious to know why they must wear mittens, they continue to believe that King Friday must have a good reason for making the rule. Lady Elaine is the only one who expresses any doubt.

The seconds tick by and then, apparently from out of nowhere, a cold breeze begins to blow. King Friday announces that this is the "hand-freezing breeze" that his special sources told him was coming. He issued the proclamation to save his subjects from getting their hands frozen.

King Friday looks at Lady Elaine, the only one without mittens, and asks her, "So, how do you feel now, Lady Elaine? The next time, you should listen to your king." Lady Elaine replies that the next time, the king should "tell us why we should listen." Then she heads home to get her mittens.

- How could King Friday have shown his concern better? Is making rules fundamentally incompatible with showing love and concern for others?
- Why did Handyman Negri neglect to ask King Friday why the rule was made about wearing mittens? Why did everyone assume that King Friday "must have a good reason" for making the rule?
- Did the rule that King Friday made have a good and loving reason behind it? Lady Elaine is the only one who questioned it. Does she remind you of anyone? Have you ever acted the part of Lady Elaine? Have you ever acted the part of King Friday or Handyman Negri?
- Have you ever seen a similar situation in an organization with which you are familiar?
- Who makes the rules in the organizations with which you are familiar? How are they enforced? What are the consequences or penalties, if any, for breaking or ignoring a rule?

- In answering the preceding questions, the reader is urged to bear in mind that a family is an organization. Indeed, it is the first organization with which all of us are familiar and the one by which we are also heavily influenced. The experiences we had with our first organization influence strongly how we view and react to all the subsequent organizations with which we come in contact. It is important to ask yourself, when you were growing up, how were the rules made in your family? Who primarily made them? What happened if you broke a rule? Were the rules explained?

CHAPTER 3

Creativity

> Play is the expression of our creativity, and creativity, I believe, is at the very root of our ability to learn, to cope and to become whatever we may be.
>
> —Fred Rogers

The Bass Violin Festival

One day in the NMB, King Friday receives a message from the Mayor of Southwood, an adjoining locality, saying that she would like to arrange a festival that involves all four of the surrounding neighborhoods. King Friday likes the idea and immediately proclaims that it will be a bass violin festival. Chuck Aber, one of his subjects, points out that He the King is the only one who actually plays the bass violin. Undaunted by the reminder, King Friday says, "Oh, so I am. Well, it looks like I will have a very large audience."

The subjects of the NMB are pleased about the prospect of a joint neighborhood festival but quite taken aback at the news that it will be just a bass violin festival and that they must all participate. Lady Aberlin is particularly disconcerted when King Friday presents her with a bass violin and describes it as "a fine instrument" that was made by an excellent instrument maker. She acknowledges that it may indeed be a very special bass violin; however, she admits to him that she absolutely cannot play the bass violin. She tells him that "just because a person has a fine instrument doesn't mean that the person can play it well." King Friday simply tells her to keep on practicing.

Over the next few days, the various characters meet to share their frustrations about being required to perform a skill that they do not have. During one of their discussions, Lady Elaine Fairchilde arrives and tells them that she has a solution to the problem. She produces her accordion, the instrument that she can play very well, which is covered by a false front to make it look like a bass violin. She tells the others that she will play her bass violin for them. They watch and listen in amazement until Lady Aberlin points out that she is actually playing her accordion. Lady Elaine acknowledges that it is indeed her accordion, but since it now *looks* like a bass violin, it could work for a bass violin festival.

Lady Elaine's clever solution gives the others an important idea: They could all think of ways to make what they do well look like a bass violin so that they could contribute to the festival.

Lady Aberlin knows how to dance, so she decides to dance with the bass violin. Miss Paulifficate puts on a costume to make her look like a bass violin—she literally plays at being a bass violin. Keith and James Michael Jones from the adjoining neighborhood of Southwood make bass violin puppets and plan to perform a bass violin "conversation."

Another neighbor plans to be a very special flower to decorate the puppet performance—she will be a "bass violet." Old Goat decides to recite a poem about the bass violin.

In the midst of their excitement about their plans, they realize that King Friday needs to be told what they are going to do and they become a little worried that he may not like the news. Lady Aberlin confides her concern to Daniel Tiger. Daniel helps her reach the conclusion that the best thing to do is simply tell the king the truth, that not everybody can learn to play the bass violin, so they are going to do other things with it, things they can do well. With the support and encouragement of all her friends, Lady Aberlin tells King Friday the truth. He listens to the plan and concludes that these are very clever ideas and that the festival could turn out to be something very special.

And indeed it is a very special bass violin festival with everyone contributing his or her own very special talent.

- What does the fable mean to you? What does it say about creativity?

- Did King Friday encourage his subjects to participate creatively in the festival? What could he have done differently?
- Think about the meaning behind King Friday giving Lady Aberlin a brand new bass violin and simply telling her to keep on practicing. What does this action say to Lady Aberlin? What does it say about King Friday's leadership style?
- Consider the different ways that the subjects came up with to contribute to the bass violin festival. Were they creative in how they reframed the king's assignment? Why or why not?
- Are you able to be creative in the same ways that the characters in the story are? Why? why not?
- What do the organizations with which you are familiar do to foster or inhibit creativity? If you currently work for an organization, what could you do to help your team members or your organization be more creative?

CHAPTER 4

Communication

In times of stress, the best thing we can do for each other is to listen with our ears *and* our hearts and to be assured that our questions are just as important as our answers.

—Fred Rogers

The Reluctant Ring-Bearer

There is great excitement in the Neighborhood of Make-Believe as everyone prepares for the wedding of Betty Templeton and James Michael Jones. King Friday will preside, Lady Aberlin and Lady Elaine Fairchilde will be bridesmaids, and Daniel Tiger has been asked to be the ring bearer. The wedding is only a few days away when Lady Aberlin learns that Daniel is reluctant to do the job. He says that he can't do it because he is unable to balance the ring on the pillow. He keeps dropping it. Betty Templeton, the bride-to-be, decides that she and Lady Aberlin should have a talk with him.

They find Daniel quite distressed. He tells them that he just can't be a ring-bearer. He says that every time he picks up the pillow, the ring falls off, and every time he thinks about being the ring-bearer, he feels worse.

Betty Templeton listens and says that this problem can be solved. She and Lady Aberlin take a small piece of tape and use it to tape the ring to the pillow. They show Daniel that now the ring cannot fall off.

Daniel replies that now the "ring" part feels better, but the "bear" part still feels bad. He says that he just doesn't want to be a ring bear and he doesn't want to wear a bear costume. He is afraid of bears. He just wants to be a tiger, not a bear.

Betty Templeton and Lady Aberlin are surprised. They tell him that he has misunderstood something very important. They explain to him the difference between being a *bear* and being a *bearer*. Daniel is so relieved. Now he can participate in the wedding without being afraid.

- Fred often said that if we wanted to know why a certain person was mean, angry, or sad, then we had to know their story, what made them what they are, and what was going in their lives at the present. What are your stories? Do you know the stories of the people with whom you work or come in contact with daily? Again, if you work, can you share personal stories in your organization, among your friends?
- Why was Daniel unable to articulate his real fear?
- When Lady Aberlin and Betty Templeton taped the ring so it wouldn't slip, they thought they had solved Daniel's problem. But they hadn't. What could Lady Aberlin and Betty Templeton have done to help Daniel express his real fear sooner and better?
- Think about this quote from Fred and how it may apply to the story: "Listening is a very active awareness of the coming together of at least two lives. Listening, as far as I'm concerned, is certainly a prerequisite of love. One of the most essential ways of saying 'I love you' is being a receptive listener."

CHAPTER 5

Consciousness

Take good care of that part of you where your best dreams come from, that invisible part of you that allows you to look upon yourself and your neighbor with delight.
—Fred Rogers

Once Upon Each Lovely Day

One day while doing his weekly trash collection, Handyman Negri realizes that a serious problem is developing. He notices that more and more trash is accumulating so that the town dump is in danger of reaching its capacity and overflowing. While the situation is not quite yet a full-blown problem, he decides that he has to bring what could develop into a serious problem to King Friday's attention before it is too late.

Handyman Negri goes to the castle expecting that King Friday will want to know his reason for requesting an audience with the king. Instead, as soon as King Friday arrives, he announces that he wants to "play a little music together." When Handyman Negri explains that he is in the midst of his weekly trash collection and that he needs to get back to work, King Friday simply says, "Well, you're not too busy at the moment for a little music." The king then pulls out several copies of a composition and suggests that they play it together. Again, Handyman Negri tries to object, saying, "Yes, I have my guitar, but I am busy. It is my job to collect all the garbage." In his most kingly fashion, King Friday says, "Garbage can wait. Music comes first!"

Handyman Negri cannot defy the king. He reaches for a copy of the composition and notices that there is a large stack of duplicates. "Are you expecting more people to come and play since you've made so many copies?" "No," explains King Friday, "I asked for two copies but the copier made 200. You can take the other 198 copies to the trash collection." Handyman Negri is shocked at the wastefulness, but he cannot speak back to the king.

They play music together. At the end of the piece, Handyman Negri again reminds King Friday that he needs to get back to his job. "Oh, let's just play it one more time," says King Friday. Handyman Negri has no choice. "Well, OK. You are the King and you are the boss."

Bob Dog, wheeling another container of garbage, comes by as they are wrapping up the second musical set. Bob Dog comments on the amount of garbage that is accumulating. King Friday doesn't seem to notice what Bob Dog has said. He simply thanks Handyman Negri for the musical interlude and hands the extra copies of the score to Handyman Negri telling him to take them to the garbage. As the king departs, Bob Dog says with dismay that he can't believe that King Friday is throwing music away. Mr. McFeely stops by and offers to take the extra copies because he can use the paper for another purpose. As they talk, Mr. McFeely tells them that the problem is very serious; he has learned that the dump at Someplace Else is now completely full. They will have to find another place for the garbage. They all agree that they need to speak with both King Friday and Queen Sara Saturday and ask for their help. In the meantime, each of them tries to find solutions by talking with the neighbors and looking for another place to put garbage.

Over the next few days, the garbage problem gets worse and worse. Two residents of Someplace Else design and build a fence to keep the garbage from overflowing into their farm and the school. More and more barrels of trash are lined up in front of the castle and around the neighborhood. Things are starting to smell. King Friday has given all of his subjects colorful nose muffs to help block out the bad smells. In fact, he has commanded that the local rocket factory run by Hilda Dingleborder stop making rockets and fill orders for nose muffs as fast as they can. Everyone finds the nose muffs terribly uncomfortable. Lady Aberlin confronts King Friday about the nose muffs saying that what they need to do is *solve* the garbage problem. King Friday responds by giving her the "honor of finding a new dump." When Lady Aberlin looks at him in shock, he replies, "Isn't that an exciting assignment. I thought you'd love it! You always love a challenge, Niece Aberlin. May I say in advance that I am very proud of you." And off he goes.

Lady Aberlin asks for ideas from others around the neighborhood. Although others are willing to help, no one knows what to do. Lady Elaine Fairchilde suggests that they put all the garbage into an airplane and send it away to *Just Anywhere*. Lady Aberlin reminds her that *Just Anywhere* might not want it either. Lady Elaine has another idea: throw it all in the ocean because the ocean is plenty big enough for everything. They conclude that neither of these ideas is very good.

As the garbage piles grow and the smell gets worse, King Friday gives Handyman Negri the job of fanning the fumes up into the sky so it won't smell so bad on the ground. He fans and fans until his arms are aching. King Friday brings him a new tool that he calls "an arm-saving device, a fan that works by itself." Handyman Negri is glad to have a battery-operated fan, but once again he knows that this is only a temporary solution.

Lady Aberlin checks with every surrounding neighborhood only to learn that there is no room for the garbage from the NMB. The only hope is the village of Northwood, and two of its citizens are on their way for a meeting. Meanwhile, Lady Elaine has another suggestion. She suggests that they reach out to people everywhere for ideas by going on the "Universe Today" television program. Everyone agrees that this is a good idea. When they tell King Friday the idea, he says that he will prepare to be on television by preparing a speech and practicing his bass violin in case they ask him to perform.

Arrangements are made for an announcement on *Universe Today*. King Friday is not asked to play his bass violin or to give a speech. He is simply asked to describe the garbage problem. Soon a response comes from a team of goats who say they can help by consuming some of the garbage. Hilda Dingleborder says that if her factory can stop making nose muffs, they will invent a machine that recycles paper, thereby reducing the amount of garbage that needs to go to a dump. The citizens of Northwood arrive and say that since the amount of garbage will be reduced through the combination of the goats consuming some and the invention recycling some, their dump can handle what is left. The citizens of the NMB eagerly go to work putting the plans into effect.

- What is the connection between the fable and consciousness? Which characters displayed consciousness: alertness, cognizance, and mindfulness? Which characters displayed denial and dismissal?
- Is there a crisis brewing in the kingdom? What role does the king play in dealing with the crisis? Does he deal with the crisis or exacerbate it?
- What does it take to deal with the crisis, and who takes the lead in dealing with it?
- How do the organizations with which you are familiar handle crises? How about those organizations that you've read about in the news, heard about on TV, or know about through the Internet? Do they ignore crises until the "smell" gets too bad? What could you do to help the organizations with which you come in contact with, or work for, better prepare for and respond to crises?
- Consider how the quote at the beginning of the chapter—"that invisible part of you that allows you to look upon yourself and your neighbor with delight"—and the following quote from Fred tie the story together. How does this in particular apply to the story?

> The values we care about the deepest, and the movements within society that support those values, command our love. When those things that we care about so deeply become endangered, we become engaged. And what a healthy thing that is! Without it, we would never stand up and speak out for what we believe.

CHAPTER 6

Courage

One of the greatest paradoxes about omnipotence is that we need to feel it early in life, and lose it early in life, in order to achieve a healthy, realistic, yet exciting sense of potency later on.
—Fred Rogers

Daniel Tiger and the Snowstorm

A big snowstorm hits the Neighborhood of Make-Believe. It snows cereal! The cereal falls so fast that it nearly covers everything. In fact, it almost reaches to the top of the clock where Daniel Tiger lives. Daniel is worried and scared that his home will be completely covered. He decides to leave his home and to wait in the castle until the storm is over.

Everyone is eager for the snow to stop. King Friday provides his subjects with cereal-proof armor and blankets to help them battle the unusual snow. He even issues a proclamation that everyone should come out to "have the honor of watching us battle the cereal." When they reach the site of the mountain of cereal that now covers Daniel's clock, they try using their tools to stop the falling cereal, but nothing seems to work. King Friday, in his most kingly manner, *commands* that the cereal stop! Still, it keeps on falling. King Friday is shocked that the cereal "had no respect for authority!" While he is expressing his frustration, Neighbor Aber finds a note saying that the snow will stop only when the one who lives in the clock is brave enough to return to his home. Everyone understands what this means; Daniel, who is so afraid of drowning in the cereal, has to come back to the clock.

King Friday gives Lady Aberlin the assignment to insure that Daniel returns to the clock. When Lady Aberlin tells Daniel what he must do, he begs her not to make him go. He tells her that he is not brave enough to go back.

Lady Aberlin and Neighbor Aber confer on the matter and come up with an idea. They create three inflatable boats that can be slipped over their bodies to keep them from drowning in the cereal. They tell Daniel that he didn't need to go back to the clock by himself for they will go with him. Even though he is still frightened, Daniel is able to go to the clock when Lady Aberlin and Neighbor Aber go with him.

The three friends work together to get through the piles of cereal to reach Daniel's clock, where they command the snowing cereal to stop. And it does! Daniel Tiger feels very proud when everyone tells him how brave he has been, but he acknowledges that he couldn't have done it without the help of his friends.

- Have you ever felt inundated by something as mundane as cereal? What does the metaphor mean to you? Why do you think Fred chose cereal as the element of drowning?
- King Friday's solution was to command the problem go away. What kind of leadership does this represent? Where did the real leadership come from?

CHAPTER 7

Community

Whether we're giving or receiving help, each one of us has something valuable to bring to this world. That's one of the things that connects us as neighbors.
—Fred Rogers

The Neighborhood of Make-Believe

"The Story of Planet Purple" was told in the NMB many years ago to help children appreciate, as Fred put it, the "delights to be found in human differences." We are not giving anything away if we point out that the story is about the difficulties in getting on with people who are different from us. It is also about the difficulties in making important and fundamental changes.

The Story of Planet Purple

On a space mission, Lady Elaine Fairchilde discovers a planet where everything looks the same. It is a place where everything is purple. Everyone has the same purple home. The sky is purple; the cars, chairs, and streets are purple; and there are the same purple trees. In addition, all the boys are named Paul and all the girls are named Pauline, and every single panda is called Purple Panda. Everyone on Planet Purple eats purple pumpernickel pudding and talks in the same monotone voice. And everybody dreams the same dreams and has the same hopes.

When Lady Elaine Fairchilde's spaceship, which is made out of bright green leaves, lands on Planet Purple, she steps out in her white astronaut suit. The Planet Purple people run and hide because they have never seen anything like her before. But one Paul, Pauline, and Purple Panda did not run and hide. They stayed around to look at this curious creature.

Lady Elaine's favorite color happens to be purple. As a result, she turns her spaceship around and flies back to tell everyone in the NMB about the intriguing planet she has discovered. Lady Elaine doesn't know that Paul, Pauline, and Purple Panda watch where she is going and decide to follow her.

Now, the Purple way to travel is just by thinking, and thinking alone. On Planet Purple, all you have to do is to think that you're someplace and instantly you'll be there. So Paul, Pauline, and Purple Panda think about Lady Elaine and where she is, and immediately they arrive in the NMB.

They can hardly believe what they see and hear. Everything and everybody is different! Purple Panda is so excited that he sits down on the first rocking chair he sees and he rocks and rocks and rocks until he remembers one of Planet Purple's laws: "Anyone who rocks on a rocking chair may not live on Planet Purple." But now, it is too late; he can never go back. He doesn't even feel sad. In fact, he secretly wonders if the reason he forgot the rule and sat down in the rocking chair and rocked was so he would have to stay in this exciting neighborhood.

Paul and Pauline decide that they do want to go back, but first they want to explore this new place. They go everywhere; they look and they listen and they sniff and they touch. In their minds, they feel the different colors, smell the different smells, and feel the different feelings. One day Paul falls down and hurts himself. He feels something wet trickling down his cheek. When Albert, the rabbit, asks him why he is crying, he has to ask what "crying" means; no one ever cries on Planet Purple. When Albert hears that Paul has never cried before, he says, "Then you've just started to live."

After a while, Paul and Pauline decide to return to Planet Purple. As soon as they think about being there, they are back home. They tell the other Pauls and Paulines about the place where Lady Elaine lives; how everything is so different and nobody is exactly the same as anyone else. They even tell about Purple Panda rocking on the rocking chair. Everyone knows he has broken the law and can never come back.

Paul and Pauline help the Planet Purple people imagine the different colors, sounds, smells, and feelings they had learned about until all the people want life to be different on Planet Purple. It takes a long time to change their planet. Some people don't like some things and other people didn't like other things, but everybody says that being different is better than being all the same all the time. They even change the law about rocking chairs so Purple Panda can come back anytime he wants.

To show their appreciation to Lady Elaine Fairchilde for helping them become different, the citizens of Planet Purple hold a celebration to announce that the name of Planet Purple will now be Planet Purple Fairchilde. Both Lady Elaine and Purple Panda come to the celebration.

- Planet Purple is placed in direct contrast to Lady Elaine's NMB. In what ways is your organization, or the ones with which you come in contact, like Planet Purple or more like the NMB?
- What are the challenges and difficulties facing Planet Purple? Is your organization, or any of which you know, facing many of the same challenges and difficulties?
- What does Fred mean when he describes the Purple way to travel as "just by thinking and thinking alone?" Likewise, why would a place like Planet Purple have a law against rocking in a rocking chair? Are there any ways and/or rules in your organization, or those you know, that are similar to these ways of traveling and these laws? If so, what do they tell you about your organization and the ones you know? Would other people agree with your interpretations? Whom would you choose to share your interpretations?

PART II

Interpretations of the Fables

CHAPTER 8

Planet Purple vs. Planet Prism

Since so many of the fables make use of Planet Purple—the one with which we ended Part I—we begin our interpretations of the fables with it.

"The Story of Planet Purple" not only is an excellent introduction to Fred's wisdom but also demonstrates how much his ideas apply to the world of work.

As we've pointed out, the story was told in the NMB many years ago to help children appreciate the "delights to be found in human differences."[1]

We want to take a deeper look at the story and what it tells us about organizations and work.

We think of Ms. Fairchilde as a highly skilled employee who has demonstrated that she is both a challenger and an adventurer. She could well be a senior vice president of a major organization.

Her current assignment is to explore different models for the design of her organization. She is very excited when she comes upon P.P., Inc. She feels that she has found something new. And she feels there is a beautiful simplicity about a place where there are no disagreements, no competition, and no differences of opinion about the long-term goals, that is, no dreams of the organization. She wants to share this discovery with her colleagues.

However, what she doesn't realize is that just by coming to P.P., Inc, in asking questions, and exploring their operations, she has already perturbed the whole system-the status quo. First of all, she arrives like an emissary from another world in an advanced energy-saving vehicle ("made of green leaves"), and she is dressed to the hilt in a white designer suit. Most members of P.P., Inc's staff want nothing to do with her. Indeed, they run and hide. But three individuals are not frightened; they are intrigued. They decide to follow her back to her corporate headquarters to learn more about the way things are done there.

Symbolically, Ms. Fairchilde has come upon an old-fashioned, overly socialized, repressive organization in which employees exist in a state of suspended or arrested psychological-emotional-development. The repressiveness of these kinds of organizations is symbolized by the lack of color. There is no diversity in them whatsoever.

Furthermore, there is a complete lack of integration between the mind and the body as the use of the "thinking way" of traveling and the rule about rocking demonstrate. Feelings and emotions are kept completely apart from thoughts and thinking in general. They are denigrated and put down altogether. Feelings and emotions are so completely inferior that they don't deserve any role at all.

The intrigue that Ms. Fairchilde feels when she first comes upon P.P., Inc. is akin to the desire that many of us have to be in a "safe cocoon," a place where we know exactly what to do and how to do it. We've all had occasion to hear someone say, "I just want to go to work and do my job; I don't want to have to deal with all that brainstorming and political stuff." These are the ones who run and hide when something new comes along. But the three individuals who decide to follow Ms. Fairchilde back to her corporate headquarters are different. They represent the kinds of people (or that part of every person) who are ready to give up the childish dream that one can live, survive, and thrive in a state of suspended development. They are ready to grow up. They are ready to integrate mind and body as illustrated by their exploration of their senses. They look, listen, smell, and touch. The power of exploring what it is to be a total, full, human being is expressed when Paul learns to cry and Albert the rabbit says, "Then you've just started to live."

When Paul and Pauline decide to return to P.P., Inc., they bring back a model for a different way to organize their workplace, indeed, their lives in general. They bring back a model in which each individual can be different. Although the staff of P.P., Inc has trouble adjusting to the changes brought back by Paul and Pauline, they realize that the changes are good, and they respect Paul and Pauline for their unique contributions to the organization.

As Fred put it:

> Transitions are almost always signs of growth, but they can bring feelings of loss. To get somewhere new, we may have to leave somewhere else behind.

Changing the culture of P.P., Inc. wasn't easy. "Some people didn't like some things and other people didn't like other things." There will always be some who take longer to embrace change (or a new level of adulthood), and there will always be some who simply resist it and choose to stay in a cocoon-like existence. For some, the preference for the cocoon-like existence may, in fact, be the right choice. However, in the world we live in today, very few Planet Purple organizations can continue to exist as they have been. Indeed, one of the major causes of BP's massive oil spill in the Gulf is the fact that BP is a prime example of a Planet Purple organization. Despite all the lip service, deep feelings as manifested in real concern for health, safety, and the environment in day-to-day operations were essentially absent.

The world today is struggling with a fundamental choice between two very different types of organizations. We call these Planet Purple and Planet Prism organizations.

Planet Prism Organizations

Planet Prism is the complete opposite of Planet Purple. The people of Planet Prism, their homes, what they eat, what they wear, and where they live are all completely different from one another. No two people are alike. Everyone and everything is a different color. Everyone has a different voice and speaks with a different cadence. Most of all, everyone has different hopes and dreams. Even the king is different. He enjoys talking with his subjects. He is not afraid to argue with them and to have them disagree with him. Indeed, he is big enough to learn from them. And unlike Planet Purple, people are allowed to rock in rocking chairs and also have and talk about their feelings. If Lady Elaine knew about this planet, there is no doubt that she would have fallen in love with it. This is where she would want to live.

In spite of all the talk to the contrary, Planet Purple organizations still dominate. They are the typical pyramidal organization with which we are all familiar. A small number of people at the top-the top dogs-control the larger body of people in the middle and at the bottom. In addition, different divisions that produce different products are put in separate, self-standing, and isolated silos. As a result, there is little contact between different parts of the organization. Only those at the top, if at all, understand how everything fits together. And yet, without having the big picture, one cannot compete successfully in the global economy. And one cannot also coordinate all the activities that are needed to protect the environment. For instance, it is almost impossible to get an organization to be nimble and embrace constant change unless someone knows how everything works, and therefore, who will and will not go along with change.

In Planet Purple organizations, depending upon which level of the hierarchy one is at, people are of course treated differently. The thing to remember is that people at the same level are treated as if they were the same, as if they were interchangeable parts of a gigantic machine, except of course when one is at the very top, the level of the princes (top executives) and the king (CEO) of the organization.

The most distinguishing mark of Planet Purple organizations is that they have a single measure of performance and success. One is not valued for who one is and what one does, but only for what one can add to "the bottom line." Everything is measured in terms of money, or something else that can be reduced to a single number, because it is regarded as the one and only true measure of the state of the organization.

In the not-so-distant past, Planet Purple organizations provided stable employment and in return earned the undying loyalty of their members. All of this has changed dramatically in recent years. Increasingly in today's world, one is merely a contract employee that can be hired and fired at will. The organization has no long-term commitment to its employees, and they have no long-term commitment and loyalty to it. The relationship with the organization is purely impersonal and based on money alone. At the end of the day, one disconnects from the organization, unplugs as it were, and goes home to a life that is completely separate from work. Work and life are strictly compartmentalized.

The Nobel-Prize-winning economist Milton Friedman is the best-known philosophical spokesperson for Planet Purple organizations. Friedman's philosophy is summed up in the single statement for which he is best known: "The sole obligation of a business is to maximize profits for its stockholders." All other considerations such as the health and the safety of its employees and their families, the well-being of the community in which it is located, and the general environment are irrelevant. In fact, for Friedman as well as for many economists, an organization's *stock*holders are the only relevant *stake*holders, meaning the only relevant parties that have a legitimate stake in the organization.

According to Friedman, the marketplace decides what's best based on the sole criterion of profitability, and that's the way it ought to decide. For instance, if a polluter is less profitable than a nonpolluter, then the marketplace is the best and the most efficient means of getting rid of the polluter. In other words, let the marketplace weed out the bad from the good. The trouble is that by the time a polluter is gotten rid of, they will have caused irreparable harm to the environment. BP is a prime example. Are we to believe that the marketplace alone will make the right decision with regard to that organization?

Planet Prism organizations are the complete opposite of the Planet Purple organization way of thinking. People are first and foremost valued for who they are. While Planet Prism organizations are interested in making money, money alone is not their sole or primary concern. They want to make products that serve authentic human needs and do no harm to the environment. They measure their success by the health and well-being of their members, their families, and their surrounding communities. Planet Prism organizations pride themselves in making sure that everyone connected with the organization has an understanding as to where they fit in the big picture. They do everything in their power to tear down the walls, physical and emotional, between different parts of the organization.

Planet Prism organizations understand that people work primarily to find meaning and purpose in their lives. Planet Prism organizations understand that by doing well for the environment and adopting socially worthy causes that improve the state of the world, they are thereby doing well for themselves as well. They understand that people want to work for organizations that do good. It makes their members feel good about themselves.

If Milton Friedman is the philosophical spokesperson, or hero, for Planet Purple organizations, then Fred Rogers is the philosophical spokesperson, or hero, for Planet Prism organizations:

> The world is so much richer because of diversity. Different members of a team play different roles ... the uniqueness of each one of us makes everyone's input valuable-in a society, a community, and a workplace. A world where everyone is different helps us to appreciate each one's uniqueness.

If Fred stood for anything, first and foremost, it was for the health, the well-being, and the general welfare of all human beings.

It is extremely difficult, if not nearly impossible, for the health of an organization to be greater than that of its least healthy members. It is certainly very difficult to be greater than the health of its least healthy top executives. And it is very difficult to be healthy in unhealthy organizations.

Fred understood that people and organizations were too complex to be reduced to a single number such as the bottom line. To reduce people and organizations to a single number is akin to saying that the development of a child can be reduced entirely to his or her height, weight, or IQ.

What Can You Do If You Are in Planet Purple Organization?

No one is right for every organization, and every organization is not right for everyone.

Many people are perfectly happy to work for Planet Purple organizations. They don't want to be part of an extended "work community or neighborhood." They just want to put in their eight hours and go home to their families. There is nothing wrong with this work philosophy.

On the other hand, we believe that a growing number of people want to work for Planet Prism organizations. They want their work to be a meaningful part of their lives, not separate from it. They want their organizations to do good because they want to be associated with good. They want their organizations to be communities and neighborhoods in the best sense of the terms.

But what if you are a Planet Prism person in a Planet Purple organization, and vice versa? What if you can't quit your job and move to an organization that is a better fit?

Seek out others within your organization that are like you and form in effect a shadow organization that can support you and your sanity. For instance, Planet Prism people in a Planet Purple organization seek out other Planet Prism people who can support them emotionally. They meditate and take yoga classes to better manage their stress. They partake freely and willingly of therapy and counseling. They do everything they can in their power to expand the Planet Prism activities in their lives.

A personal friend-call her Janet-found that she was able to create a Planet Prism workgroup within the larger Planet Purple organization for which she worked. When Janet discovered that the larger organization was dependent on her workgroup, she used that knowledge to create a climate that insulated herself and her group from the larger organization.

We are not suggesting that everyone can physically or emotionally insulate himself or herself as Janet did. We are suggesting that when an organizational culture is toxic to an individual, one can to a certain extent emotionally or psychologically buffer himself or herself from that culture. But when emotional or psychological insulation no longer works-when one can no longer take it-it is absolutely necessary to leave physically to preserve one's emotional health and well-being.

Two Methods for Changing Organizations

As we've said, changing organizations is one of the most difficult problems people and organizations face. For this reason, we want to outline very briefly two processes that we've used successfully with many organizations to help them change for themselves. It can be used on any difficult problem as well.

Twenty or so key executives and top managers are brought together and divided at random into four groups. One group is asked to defend the status quo, that is, why the organization does not need to change at all; why everything needs to stay the same. The second group is asked to explore and defend moderate change; the third, major change. And, the fourth is asked to explore and defend radical change, where nothing is the same; where everything is the complete opposite of the status quo.

It is important to note that people are assigned at random to each of the groups. It is often the case that those who don't agree with a particular position can make the strongest case for it precisely because they are not completely taken in by it. Also, it is very important for each position along the full spectrum of change, or problem-solving alternatives, to have its full day in court so that later there will not be objections that the process was biased against the status quo. After all, each group, regardless of where they are along the spectrum of change, will develop some valuable and worthwhile contributions to the analysis. The range of ideas will be worth preserving.

After each group has developed its best case and made a presentation to all of the others, four new groups are also formed at random. Each new group is now asked, "Given that you've heard the various cases for different degrees and kinds of change, what's best for the *organization*? What do you recommend that *you* do next? What, if anything, do you suggest be accepted and incorporated from each of the groups?" In this way, each of the four groups potentially comes up with a new and different plan of action.

After the new plans have been debated, the group as a whole is then asked to vote on which plan it believes makes most sense, and most important of all, how they will implement it. At this point in the process, the members of the group have, because of what they've already explored and debated, a better basis for modifying their plans.

The second method makes use of Figure 8.1.

Once again, people are divided into four groups at random. Each group is then asked to fill out Figure 8.1. That is, in every organization, there are always some things we would like to preserve, that is, keep the same-the status quo. And, there are always some things that need to change. In addition, some things will be easy to keep the same or change and others will be difficult.

The task is not only to fill out Figure 8.1 but also to indicate how one will achieve Transformative Leadership, the most difficult

Figure 8.1 Change Management Versus Leadership

thing to obtain. That is, should one go after easy wins first, that is, Preservative Managership, and only then attempt change?

As we shall see, the processes that we've outlined earlier in this chapter are dependent upon all of Fred's principles if they are to work properly.

We need to note, however, that as much as the status quo needs to be heard, it is more tenuous than ever in today's world. Thomas L. Friedman and Michael Mandelbaum quote one interviewee for their book, *That Used To Be Us,* as follows:

> We want people who have a completely open mind... and then the ability to learn constantly and challenge the status quo-no matter what the level of the company where they are employed. Challenging the status quo is the most critical thing because if your employees don't challenge your status quo, someone else's employees will and they will disrupt the status quo before you do.[2]

Concluding Remarks

The deepest beliefs of Planet Purple organizations are as follows (notice that these beliefs are so taken for granted that most people and organizations don't even know that they have them; that's why when people are given the opportunity to surface deeply held beliefs, these will be among the first to be challenged in the processes outlined in the previous section):

1. To attain the illusion of complete control, one must give up uniqueness; everyone must think, act, and be the same.

2. One must be disconnected from one's body and feelings; that's why rocking, let alone crying, was not permitted on Planet Purple.
3. One must believe that everything, for example, space travel, can be accomplished through thinking alone; once again, one must be disconnected from one's feelings. In other words, only thinking matters.

In contrast, Planet Prism organizations are the epitome of integration and connectedness between our brains, our bodies, our feelings, and our souls and spirits.

CHAPTER 9

Good Friends

There are at least three important messages in the story of "Good Friends" that are applicable to adult life. The first is about learning to listen for the feelings behind the words. The words a colleague uses when he or she is stressed may not actually describe the pain he or she is really feeling. Daniel kept asking Lady Aberlin to explain *why* she had forgotten him, but what he really wanted to know was *how* could he trust their friendship if he could so easily be forgotten. When Lady Aberlin stops offering logical explanations and hears Daniel's deep feeling and articulates it for him, this is the point when he can relax and let go of his anger.

The second important message is about *learning to accurately name our feelings*. When we accurately name a feeling, we can react in a more appropriate manner. When Lady Aberlin told Daniel about the time a friend forgot to come to her birthday party, Daniel asked if she felt mad about her friend forgetting. Lady Aberlin clarifies for Daniel that what she felt was not anger but *disappointment*. This clarification is very important because how one reacts to disappointment is very different from how one reacts to anger. Learning to name feelings, to recognize the subtle distinctions between, for example, anxiety and fear or guilt and shame, is an important aspect of emotional intelligence. If we haven't learned to make distinctions between basic feelings, we are likely to react inappropriately and escalate emotional situations.

The third important message in the story is about identifying the triggering feeling. Identifying triggering feelings can help us appropriately label the emotion being felt. When something happens that causes us to feel angry—for example, Daniel's presenting emotion to Lady Aberlin was anger—however, when, with Lady Aberlin's help, he stopped to retrace the situation to locate the triggering event, he discovered that what he felt was abandonment. A technique for identifying triggering feelings is to engage in a process that we call "rewind your mind." This entails stepping back long enough to play the situation backward to the point at which emotions began to take over. When that moment is discovered, we can often label the feeling and react more appropriately. Learn to rewind your mind and help your colleagues do it also. It can help to take some of the "heat" out of the workplace.

The story "Good Friends" also illustrates that talking about difficult feelings can be therapeutic. For instance, to help children manage their fears regarding difficult issues such as death and divorce, one needs to allow them to discuss these issues in ways that are less threatening. In other words, children need to connect with others so that they can express their deepest fears, joys, hopes, and dreams. The same applies to adults although it is often more difficult for adults to connect and express deep feelings than it is for children to do so.

Adults Have the Same Needs

As we stated earlier in this chapter, adults have the same need to connect with others. Leading organizations, what we are calling Planet Prism organizations, have learned how to address this need in innovative ways. For instance, employees regularly get together to read and to share different books on human development, individual and organizational health, and important social issues. They don't just read books about business. They read and talk about people.

Planet Prism organizations regularly invite nationally recognized experts in management to spend at least a full day interacting with employees, customers, and other major stakeholders, in order to gain an outside perspective and a critique of the organization. Prior to their arrival, employees are encouraged to read and to discuss the work and ideas of the incoming experts in small groups. By inviting outsiders with different and conflicting points of view, the organizations are continually open to new ideas.

An Example

Donna worked as the head of broadcast standards for a major TV network. She had the responsibility for insuring that the content of children's TV programs was not only age appropriate, but also actually aided children's health and development. The programs certainly were not supposed to cause harm.

Donna struggled constantly with getting the producers and writers of children's TV programs to go along with her mandate. They just wanted to produce and to write exciting shows that would "bring in the numbers," that is, the audience. Bringing in the numbers, the bottom line, was the only thing that really mattered.

Then the horrific Columbine shootings occurred. Because they were so tragic, they provided a teachable moment to reach the producers and writers. They provided an opportunity to connect with the writers and producers about the importance of making shows that helped young children to grow and to develop in healthy ways.

After the Columbine shootings, Donna invited leading experts on the development of boys, such as William Pollack,[1] to conduct a one-day training seminar. The purpose of the seminar was to expose the producers and the writers of children's television programs to the issues that young children, especially boys, struggle with, and consequently to help explain why horrific events such as Columbine occur.

We believe that the principle of connectedness, or reaching out, needs to be continually encouraged and broadened—with both children and adults. The list of mentors, coaches, and outside influences that workers and managers are exposed to should be expanded to include experts on male and female psychology and emotional development so that everyone can continue to grow. In this way our organizations can truly become learning and growing neighborhoods.

Concluding Remarks

Planet Prism organizations incorporate connectedness in deep and meaningful ways. It is deeply embedded in and is a fundamental part of their everyday operations. They use connectedness as their primary criterion in selecting prospective members. For instance, on a cross-country flight on Southwest Airlines (SWA), Ian struck up a conversation with one of the flight attendants. She confirmed that SWA does indeed select for attitude, and train for skills. She also described in detail SWA's hiring process.

SWA's selection process begins by inviting prospective members to attend a meeting with thirty or so other people. Prospective members are asked open-ended questions, such as "Tell me about a time when you went beyond what was expected of you as part of your normal job." While the interviewers are certainly interested in the verbal responses to the questions, they are even more interested in nonverbal responses. They are looking for the demonstrated ability of prospective members to connect instantly in a group of complete strangers.

The flight attendant noted that when she started the selection process, nearly 240,000 people applied for a job with SWA. At the end, only 1600 were actually hired. That's only two-thirds of 1 percent of all those that applied initially.

SWA's selection process is at the heart of the "select for attitude; train for skills" philosophy, and it represents the future of all companies. This is the model for Planet Prism organizations.

No matter what their main products or services are, all companies are now in the service business. Zappos Shoes is just one example of a business that understands this point of view. Everyone needs to connect with customers and to one another both in and outside of the organization.

In an August 28, 2011, interview by Adam Bryant in *The New York Times,* Andy Lansing, CEO of the Chicago-based Levy Restaurants, stated that when interviewing a senior member of the company for a new position, Levy's first question is, "are you nice?" Levy believes being nice and being successful are strongly connected in business. He admitted his approach to hiring is fairly nontraditional. As he put it: "... the reactions are priceless. There's usually a long pause, like they are waiting for me to smile.... And then I say, 'No, seriously, are you nice?' " Otherwise, he tells them, they are applying to the wrong company.

CHAPTER 10

No Bare Hands in This Land

The moral of the story is that you can't just command and order people around. If we let people know why the rules are necessary, then they are much more likely to go along with them. Even more important, people need to participate in the making of the rules.

"No Bare Hands in This Land" illustrates that in today's world of highly educated workers, the CEO—the King!—can't just issue rules and edicts at will and expect them to be followed blindly. Today's CEOs have to explain the purpose for the rules. *Rules that don't make sense are senseless.*

Good organizations not only make good rules *for* their members but also make them *with* their members.

A Common Misperception

There is a common misperception of Fred Rogers. Many people think that because he was thoroughly genuine and loving, caring and accepting, he was, therefore, permissive toward children's behavior, that he advocated no rules, discipline, or limits when it came to raising children. Nothing could be further from the truth. In fact, Fred described discipline as "a loving gift" that parents gave to their children when they needed it.

Fred understood that children desperately need and want limits and rules. Furthermore, they need and want appropriate discipline, but not hurtful or harmful discipline.

Fred knew that we showed our love for our children through demonstrating what was expected of them and what the consequences were if they didn't meet those expectations. *To think that healthy children and adults would result without sensible rules and appropriate discipline goes against every grain of research on children.*

In Planet Prism organizations, the rules emerge from all of the stakeholders.[1]

For instance, members with appropriate help from the outside, for example, consultants who are experts in organizational behavior, formulate the rules for conducting meetings and for dealing with difficult people. In this way, the rules are anything but abstract, academic, cold, and impersonal. The rules cover not only how to run meetings efficiently and effectively, but also how to encourage and to maintain civility. In formulating the rules, it is assumed that the feelings of everyone connected with the organizations are paramount. Above all, the rules are held to an absolute minimum.

Planet Prism organizations have clear-cut rules regarding employee misconduct, aggressiveness, and violence in the workplace.[2]

From day one, Planet Prism organizations make it perfectly clear that sexually offensive jokes or those featuring violence will not be tolerated for one instant. Statements such as "I'm so mad at you that I'm going to hit you!" or "You deserve to be thrashed" or "Get out of my face or else!" are taken very seriously. "I was just kidding" is not accepted as an excuse. They have a "zero tolerance policy" with regard to sexual harassment and workplace violence. Anyone violating these rules is sent immediately to HR and counseling to determine whether he or she is still fit to remain in the organization.

Of course, by now, most people and most organizations are well aware of sexual harassment, and we believe that they are seriously trying to put an end to it. However, organizations are now faced with a new and perhaps even more insidious concern.

Because they have become such a problem, we want to discuss a particular set of issues that are particularly troubling in today's organizations. Unfortunately, although Planet Prism organizations do everything in their power to eliminate the issues through selecting the proper members, they still suffer from them as well. We are referring to the disturbing rise of rudeness and incivility throughout society as a whole.

It is estimated that at least 20 to 25 percent of people leave their jobs each year because their organizations refuse even to recognize rudeness and incivility, let alone to do anything serious about it. Because it is so costly to replace and to train skilled people, this means that organizations are paying a heavy price for not doing anything serious about rudeness and incivility.

The best organizations have clear-cut policies and rules with regard to rudeness and incivility:[3]

- They have zero tolerance policies; that is, they make it perfectly clear that rudeness and incivility will not be tolerated under any circumstances. One instance is one too many.
- They take an honest look in the mirror; that is, they ask themselves, "What is it about our culture that has encouraged or turned a blind eye toward incivility; do we promote in subtle and not-so-subtle ways those who are rude; in other words, are we to blame?"
- They weed out trouble before it enters their organization; that is, they ask prospective members for their permission to talk with previous employers; they probe for underlying reasons why the person left their previous position. They ask the prospective member whether they will allow them to ask their previous employer questions with regard to rudeness and incivility.
- They teach civility. It is not enough to be *against* rudeness and incivility; to root it out, one has to be *for* something positive, that is, civility.
- They put their ear to the ground and listen carefully for any signs that incivility and rudeness are taking root in their organization.
- When incivility occurs, they react immediately and forcefully; they don't wait for days to pass before they respond to uncivil acts; the goal is a "just in time" policy with regard to positive and to negative behaviors.
- They heed early warning signals. Acts of incivility send out early warning signals long before they occur, in forms such as increased absenteeism and workplace sabotage. The best organizations are constantly on the lookout for early warning signs of rudeness and incivility.

- They don't make excuses for powerful instigators of incivility; that is, the higher a person is in the organization, the less tolerance he or she has with regard to incivility. This policy is important because research has shown that incivility tends to travel downward. In unhealthy organizations, those on top are uncivil toward insubordinates, but of course not vice versa.
- They invest heavily in post-departure interviews. Again, it is estimated that annually anywhere between 20 and 25 percent of people leave organizations each year because of rudeness and incivility. There is no doubt that rudeness and incivility seriously hamper the bottom line. Exit interviews are a valuable way of taking a final look in the mirror.

Concluding Remarks

Good neighborhoods have good rules that people respect and understand. For instance, every one of us has a basic responsibility to nip rudeness and incivility at its core.

This doesn't mean that everyone necessarily agrees with all of the rules all of the time. Again, Fred Rogers said it well:

> Call them rules or call them limits, good ones, I believe, have this in common They serve reasonable purposes; they are practical and within [a person's] capability; they are consistent; and they are an expression of loving concern.

CHAPTER 11

The Bass Violin Festival

Everyone can relate to the story of the "The Bass Violin Festival." At some time or other, all of us have been given assignments that seem unreasonable. But there are deeper lessons to be learned when we examine the story as a metaphor for the workplace.

The story starts with the CEO, King Friday, announcing to the staff, that is, his subjects, that he has received a proposal from a complimentary organization, represented by the Mayor of Southwood, for a partnership. It is clear that the CEO wants the partnership to proceed. It is also clear that the king wants NMB, Inc. to be the lead company. As a result, all of the subjects must develop a plan to make the king's expertise the central element of the partnership. The subjects (i.e., the staff) are dubious because they realize that the CEO is the sole true expert in NMB's technology. They also realize intuitively that NMB's technology is not, in and of itself, sufficient for the proposed partnership. Their frustration is exacerbated when the CEO presents one senior staff member with a newer version of the technology and thinks that this "fine instrument" is what is needed to jump start the process.

With this act, King Friday commits a mistake that is common in the thinking of far too many organizations. This is the mistaken belief that newer and better technology is always the solution to every problem. In fact, research has shown time and again the complete opposite. Technology alone without the skills, knowledge, and confidence to use it will not succeed. In fact, technology by itself often increases our fears and makes us painfully aware of our shortcomings. Instead of putting us more at ease and making us more proficient, it increases our fears and anxieties, as it did with Lady Aberlin.

Furthermore, adopting a single solution to a complex problem as King Friday did leads to the commission of a mistake that is fundamental to creative problem solving. The mistake, or error, is *solving the wrong problem precisely.*

Solving the wrong problem precisely is referred to as the error of the third kind. The concept of the error of the third kind is described in the literature on strategic planning, although it is rarely discussed even there. When organizations fixate on a single solution to a complex problem as King Friday did and as many organizations do when they rely on a single product or narrow mission, they miss the opportunity to step back and check on whether they have asked the right questions in the first place. Engaging in the process of formulating and redefining problems often results in new and creative solutions to them. In other words, like the characters in "The Bass Violin Festival," people in organizations need to take the time to play with the definition of what the true problems really are, or like the characters in our story, the redefinition of the word "play."

Fred Rogers often talked about the important contribution to human development that comes from play:

> One way to think about play is as the process of finding new combinations for known things—combinations that may yield new forms of expression, new inventions, new discoveries, and new solutions. I like thinking about play in this way because it gives play some of the importance it deserves.

A CEO that is fortunate to have a staff like the characters in the NMB has much to be thankful for. Lady Elaine Fairchilde, Lady Aberlin, Miss Pullificate, and the others redefined the problem and came up with a wide range of creative approaches to the concept of a bass violin festival. And just as important, the fact that they each found a solution drawn from their individual talents and expertise led to greater involvement and investment in the outcome than does a single, imposed solution.

Let us recount the lessons of "The Bass Violin Festival":

1. Technology alone is never a substitute for skill. The best bass violin in the world, that is, technology, will not make up for the fact that we don't know how to use the technology, that is, play the violin.
2. By itself, technology often increases our fears. It makes us painfully aware of our shortcomings. Instead of putting us more at ease, it increases our fears and anxieties. It makes us feel very uneasy.
3. Often when we are afraid—indeed the more that we are afraid—we project our fears onto others. Instead of owning up to our fears as our own, we blame others. It is easy, and even justified, to blame the predicament entirely on King Friday. After all, he was the one who gave his subjects a seemingly impossible task. But King Friday is not basically responsible for the fears that the subjects feel with regard to their creative ideas. For all that we know, the king intentionally wanted to give his subjects a task that he knew they couldn't complete to see if it would stimulate their creativity and help them overcome their fears.
4. Creativity also forces us to confront our deepest fears: Are we good enough? Are we liked for who we are? Will we look foolish and be laughed at if we expose our ideas and feelings to the world? Will I be punished and ridiculed for my ideas? Through creativity, we discover the fears really lie within us and not outside the world.
5. In many myths and fairytales, most often it is the youngest child or the feeblest member of the community, the one who is undeveloped or handicapped in some way, who demonstrates the courage to tell the truth. Where older children and adults have learned to be wary of the world—in far too many cases, beaten down by it—the youngest child or most disenfranchised citizen has not learned to distrust his or her inner voice and creativity. The child's innocence or the disenfranchised individual's point of view is seen as a protective barrier against the harshness of the world.
6. To be creative, we have to be a child again. We have to be childlike without being childish.

Creativity: To See the World Again as a Child

All of us are creative. All of us are artists. We just need to take refresher courses to remind us from time to time.

A few years ago, a company sent its entire team of top executives to an outside course in creativity. A prominent feature of the course was a module that consisted of going to an art museum and looking at the paintings under the guidance of a docent. Prior to their actual participation in the course, this particular module elicited the most negative response of all the parts of the program. After all, what does going to an art museum have to do with business? However, after they took it, all of the executives agreed that it was the most valuable part of the entire program. Why? Because it allowed them to look at familiar things with fresh eyes. The docent taught the executives how to look at modern art through the eyes of the artists. This allowed them to better understand what the artists were trying to do.

Like most people, the executives had to be taught to look at modern art. They needed to understand that modern artists are not trying to be like cameras. They are after a deeper reality. They are trying to get us all to look at everyday things in totally different new and different ways. To accomplish this, they often have to shock us out of old ways of doing and seeing things. For instance, as Fred Rogers asked us, "Why can't trees be purple? Why can't people be green?" They were when we were children. This is precisely why in 1905 the painting by Matisse of a woman with a purple tinged face caused such a tremendous uproar in French society. He upset the adult conventions with regard to painting—the status quo—of the time.

To see the world again as a child is the fundamental basis of creativity. Creativity involves total immersion in one's work. Even more important, it involves feelings of joy, fun, and play.

One of Fred Rogers' most profound observations is that our play and creativity are two of the truest and most powerful windows into our innermost feelings.

In order for organizations to have access to the creative potential of their members, they need to integrate play with work. In other words, they need to think *systemically* about how play and work influence each other and how the integration between play and work impacts the health of our businesses and our very lives.

The late Russell Ackoff, one of the premier systems thinkers of our time, put it this way:

> Perhaps the most costly [breakup] in which our culture has been engaged is the [separation] of life itself into work, play, learning, and inspiration. Each of these aspects of life has been separated from the others by creating institutions for engaging in only one at a time, excluding the other three as much as possible. Businesses are designed for work, not play, learning or inspiration. Country clubs, theaters, and sports stadiums are designed for play, not work, learning or inspiration. Schools are designed for learning, not work, play, or inspiration. Museums and churches are designed for inspiration, not work, play, or learning. However, one of the most important [we would say "spiritual"] products of systems thinking is the realization that the effectiveness with which any of these four functions can be carried out depends on the extent to which they are carried out together, in an integrated way.
>
> We will succeed in continuously improving our standard of living and quality of life only to the extent that we erase the distinctions between work, play, learning, and inspiration, and the institutions that facilitate them. Their interaction is another interaction that management must come to manage effectively.[1]

The Error of the Third Kind

As we stated earlier in this chapter, a particular concept is at the heart of creativity: the error of the third kind.[2]

The error of the third kind is the error of "solving the wrong problem or problems precisely!" For example, in "The Bass Violin Festival," a type 3 error occurs if we assume that the problem to be solved is to learn to play the bass violin, and we proceed to try to accomplish such a difficult task in an impossibly short period of time. If we do this, we are indeed attempting to solve the wrong problem precisely. Indeed, we have become hooked into solving the wrong problem.

Another form of the type 3 error occurs when we attempt to obtain the best violin in the world, that is, to solve the problem through better technology alone. Instead, the solution consists in redefining the nature of the problem as for example when we play with the meaning(s) of playing a bass violin.

But how does one ever know that one is indeed solving the wrong problems? The answer is that by ourselves we can't. We need others to inform us of our blind spots. Once again, we need to be connected to others. In "The Bass Violin Festival," different solutions emerge because there are different people in the NMB. Since they are not all alike, they each interpret the assignment differently but find the way to merge their different interpretations into one successful Festival.

Making Your Organization More Creative

The exercise for changing an organization that we described in Chapter 8 is a good device to make one's organization more creative.

Recall that the exercise begins by taking a typical group of 20 people and dividing them into four smaller groups of five each. Recall further that one group is asked to defend the status quo whatever it is, for example, why they don't need to change their current product line, business strategies, or mission statement. That is, they are asked to make the strongest argument they can as to why sticking with the tried and true ways—the status quo—is the best way to face the future. Another group is asked to depart just slightly from the status quo by embracing modest change and once again making the strongest case they can for this policy. Another group is asked to embrace major change, and the last group is asked to embrace radical change, that is, where everything is different. In effect, the last group is asked to totally reinvent the business as if it never existed in the first place.

Each group is then asked to state the assumptions they need to make so that their position is the best. Notice that one doesn't have to believe in the policy of the group to which one is assigned. (People are assigned at random.) All one has to do is go along with the assignment. Indeed, often those who disagree most with a particular policy can make the most effective case for it.

The whole point of this exercise is to produce intense debate, and it usually does. After each group has had its day in court, so to speak, new groups are formed. (Again, at random.) Each new group is asked to come up with the best plan that is based on the four presentations they have just heard. That is, what's the best they can do in the foreseeable future based on the four previous presentations? In other words, what do they want to keep (incorporate) versus throw out from the first four groups?

We have yet to see this exercise fail.

The point is that everyone needs to be encouraged to think outside of the current boxes. Even more to the point, people need ways that will actually help them to think outside of familiar boxes.

Increasing Creativity in Our Private Lives

One does not have to be a member of a group or an organization to use this technique. We have helped individuals use it in their private lives when they are facing such crucial issues as whether to change jobs, to go back to school, or even to get a divorce.

CHAPTER 12

The Reluctant Ring-Bearer

Fred Rogers was fond of saying that if we wanted to know why a certain person was mean, angry, or sad, then we had to know their story, that is, what made them what they are and what was going in their lives at the present. People don't act randomly. There are always reasons for their behavior. This is the moral of "The Reluctant Ring-Bearer."

Every person is a lifetime of stories. To truly know a person *is* to know his or her stories, for in the beginning and in the end, a person *is* the sum of his or her stories. Even better, every person is the multiplicative product of his or her stories. We say "multiplicative product" because the stories interact to influence one another. That is, the stories that define a person's life do not exist in isolation. They continually evolve, interact, and combine in a multitude of ways.

Howard Schultz, the CEO of Starbucks, often tells the story of his humble beginnings and how they relate directly to his running of the organization. Schultz grew in poor housing project. He remembers vividly the day his father, a blue-collar worker, came home early from work because he slipped on ice and injured himself. As a result of his injury, Schultz's father lost his job. Schultz never forgot the gulf between the haves and the have-nots. When he is asked why Starbucks charges three dollars for a cup of coffee, he replies, "So we can afford to pay health insurance for our hourly employees."

Planet Purple organizations don't care about the stories of their employees, but Planet Prism organizations do. The stories of their members are the social glue that binds Planet Prism organizations together.

In recent years, the Columbia School of Medicine has recognized the importance of stories in the training of doctors. To better understand their patients' needs and problems, the School of Medicine hired eminent writers to train doctors how to listen to and capture the stories of their patients. We believe that business schools need to do so the same.

Seven Basic Kinds of Stories

There are seven basic kinds of stories, which are the basic building blocks of human experience. Every person is a unique combination of these seven.

1. *Overcoming the Monsters*

Every human being has to confront his or her internal demons and to slay his or her external monsters if he or she is to become an adult.

The internal demons are many: the fear of failure, and for just as many, the fear of success. In addition, there is greed, addictive behaviors, and more.

The external monsters are just as many, for example the childhood bully, the overprotective or abusive parent, the mean sibling, the sarcastic teacher, and the intimidating boss or colleague.

Confronting and slaying one's demons and monsters does not mean literally killing them. The confrontation and slaying is more psychological than it is physical. It means that one has faced one's deepest fears and that one is no longer fully threatened by them.

One of the most important and intriguing books that anyone can ever read is *The Hero with a Thousand Faces* by Joseph Campbell. Campbell, the eminent student of world mythology, recounts that one of the most fundamental myths of all cultures worldwide is that of the hero's journey. To be a hero—psychologically to cross the threshold from adolescence to adulthood—one must battle with and defeat one's inner demons and outer monsters. For example, to win the proverbial princess, and hence to enter into marriage and adulthood, that is, to reach sexual maturity, the young boy must confront and slay the symbolic dragon. The symbolic dragon stands for the parents or the community—the status quo—that one must defeat if one is to develop in new ways. Paradoxically, only by *slaying the ways of the old community* does he prove that he is worthy of becoming its member.

2. *The Quest*

The hero's journey begins and ends with a quest. The quest is to develop the skills and the knowledge to seek out the dragon and then to slay it. In other words, the hero's initial quest is to develop his technical skills and competency so that he can hold down a job.

But the later quests, especially in the lives of men, are that of developing emotional competency. Women often face the reverse quest: developing technical skills so that they can develop technical competency. But they also have their own dragons to slay. They have to learn to slay their dragons without using sarcasm and ridicule, that is, without preying upon the feelings of others.

All of us are on a lifelong quest: to get a better job, to find a compatible mate, to raise a good family, and to become a valued member of the community.

3. *Voyage and Return*

To complete the journey, the hero and the heroine must first begin it. They must first hear the inner call that summons the candidate to the prospective journey. If he or she refuses the call then he or she will not develop emotionally and physically.

But hearing and acknowledging the call is only the first step. The journey or the voyage itself is perilous—it is full of psychological monsters and demons around every corner. It is never fully mapped out or known completely in the very beginning. Uncertainty may well be the biggest demon and dragon of all. Little wonder why many organizations stress certainty and control and organize themselves in the form of a strict hierarchal bureaucracy.

However, even this is not the most perilous part of the journey. The hero's return is, strangely enough, often the most hazardous part of all.

Those who have not been on the journey that the hero or heroine has, who have not seen and beaten the demons and the dragons that he or she has, and who have not gone through the fundamental transformation that is required cannot truly understand the new sense of being, the new world, that he or she has brought back.

This is precisely why those who have been to a life-changing seminar or talk have such difficulty in bringing the lessons back home to their organizations. They have had the experience but others have not and you cannot learn—internalize the lessons—without having had the experience directly for yourself.

4. *Rags to Riches*

Who is not familiar with the basic story of rags to riches? It is the perennial story of the child—the underdog—who, having been born into extreme poverty and by the sweat of the brow, special abilities, prowess, and brains, rises to the top as in the popular Horatio Alger stories. If one is lucky, one never forgets one's humble beginnings for if one were to do so, one would fall back into the clutches of new demons such as arrogance, greed, and pride. To do so is to lose one's humanity.

5. *Tragedy*

Into every life, a bit of tragedy must fall. Be it with the horrific death of a child, the loss of a loved one, the failure of a business, or promise unfulfilled, tragedies are an inevitable part of life. We show our humanity by grieving with the tragedies of others.

One of the greatest tragedies is to lead an unfulfilled life, not to realize one's promise or full potential. To fail is one thing, especially if it was an honest failure, but to waste one's talents is a fate worse than death.

6. *Comedy*

To laugh is truly divine. Into every life, comedy must also fall. If life has its inevitable moments of tragedy, it also has its inevitable moments of comedy and farce. To know a person is not just to share his or her moments of despair, it is also to share the moments of joy and laughter.

7. *Rebirth*

To get up off the floor and to go off one more time into the fray, to reengage old demons and dragons, to seek out new and war over new ones is the stuff of which life is made.

And with this, the circle is complete. We return to the beginning. We fight the demons once again. We conquer the monsters both within and without.

Concluding Remarks

To listen silently, without criticism, and with an open mind to the stories of others is one of the greatest gifts and joys of all.

We often see one or more of the seven generic types of stories played out around the following major life events.

- The birth or the death of a child
- The birth or the death of a loved one
- Individual stories of success, failure, tragedy, and triumph
- Tales of joy and of woe; the times when one has felt happiness and sadness
- Overcoming great obstacles
- Developing a new skill or a hobby
- Struggles with one's peers, siblings, and families
- Continually growing in one's life
- Retirement

One of the most important tasks of an organization's leaders is providing a safe and comfortable setting so that those who want to share their stories with others can do it without risk.

Listening to the stories of others without violating their space or privacy is one of the greatest gifts we can give to ourselves and to others.

How would you describe your stories? Which of the basic types listed earlier in this chapter pertain to you personally, your organization, or one with which you have frequent contact? Can you share your stories without fear in your organization? Does your organization value the stories of its members?

For further understanding, read the eloquent words of Parker J. Palmer, one who deeply understands the power of stories:

> With people who are irrevocably committed to violence, I may never find the smallest patch of common ground. Could I find one with others whose views differ sharply from mine—a small patch, perhaps but one large enough that we could stand there and talk for a while? I had reason to believe that the answer might be yes. For example, I know of daylong dialogue programs for people who differ on difficult issues like abortion where participants are forbidden from proclaiming their positions on the issue until the last hour of the day. Instead, they are coached in the art of personal storytelling and then invited to share the experiences that gave rise to their beliefs while others *simply listen* [italics in original].
>
> Hearing each other's stories, which are often stories of heartbreak, can create an unexpected bond between so-called pro-life and pro-choice people. When two people discover that parallel experiences led them to contrary conclusions, they are more likely to hold their differences respectfully, knowing that they have experienced similar forms of grief. *The more you know another person's story, the less possible it is to see that person as your enemy* [italics ours].[1]
>
> —Parker J. Palmer

We think Fred would agree with this description about the importance of knowing someone's story!

CHAPTER 13

Once Upon Each Lovely Day

The moral of "Once Upon Each Lovely Day" is that we need to both practice care for the external environment and never take the environment for granted. But there is an even deeper moral to the story: if we want to respect and care for the external environment—Nature—then we have to respect and care for our internal environment, that is, our internal nature, our attitudes toward ourselves and the world. Integrating our respect and care for both the external environment and our internal environment is an expression of spirituality.

There are other lessons that the story teaches.

For one, King Friday is certainly not connected to his subjects. Indeed, he is profoundly disconnected from them. His kingdom is on the verge of drowning in garbage, and all he wants to do is to play music. To say that he avoids the problem is a gross understatement. He not only uses music to drown out the problem but also as a major diversion. The king is narcissistic and profoundly selfish. He is anything but a spiritual leader. He is in contact with neither his own inner nature nor that of his subjects.

For another, the king doesn't listen, because he doesn't want to hear. Handyman Negri, a poor subject—a lowly employee—is begging the king to take action, to listen to and focus on a serious problem. Instead, the king passes the job off to one of his subjects, Lady Aberlin, one of his favorites. He neglects the safety, health needs of people. In terms of Maslow's needs hierarchy, the king can't even attend to the basic, safety, and health needs of his people.

King Friday's behavior is both self-centered and somewhat immature. He is certainly not proactive about environmental concerns. He will never be cited as a "green CEO!"

Until the king stops focusing entirely on himself, the kingdom is truly rotten and smelly. The nose muffs are a feeble attempt to cover up the surface of the problem by not dealing fully with it. The fans represent other feeble attempts to avoid dealing fully with the problem.

But the biggest and the most fundamental lesson of the story is that to deal with life's problems, we have to get beyond ourselves. We have to discover a bigger purpose in life. That's why the solution is discovered only when people reach out and help one another.

Problems are not and cannot be isolated any more. They touch everyone.

All of the stories that we have considered teach us that the solutions to our problems rarely, if ever, lie solely in bigger and better technology. The solutions lie fundamentally deep within us. And the deepest sense of "within" is spiritual.

Although they express it very differently from adults, children have a keen interest in spirituality, if not religion. They want to know who they are and why they are here.

And although adults may deny and ignore it, these same questions persist throughout our entire lives. All of us are searching for meaning and purpose. All of us want to know why we are here.

For Fred, the word "consciousness" was merely a stepping-stone to the deeper concept of spirituality. And if spirituality means anything, it is recognizing and treating the whole person—the whole environment—and helping us in our search for meaning and purpose.[1]

For example, at the heart of The Container Store—a prominent example of a Planet Prism organization—is a principle that is deeply spiritual: "Fill a person's whole basket." It means meeting the needs of the whole person who walks into the store.

The Container Store uses the metaphor of a person who is lost in the desert to convey this notion. The person's immediate need is water. However, the deeper need emanates from the reason why the person was in the desert in the first place, and the stress and the trauma that he or she has suffered as a result.

Once again, providing water services the person's immediate needs. But The Container Store wants to get to the deeper, underlying needs. They believe that if they meet these needs, then "the profits will follow." The *fill the whole basket* principle of The Container Store is about meeting the true and authentic needs of whole human beings.

Ian has found through his own research in organizational spirituality[2] that those organizations that practice spirituality believe in practicing it for its own sake. They believe firmly that one must not practice spirituality to make money, for personal gain, power, or the like. They believe that if they practice spirituality other than for its own sake, then profits will not follow. Conversely, if one practices spirituality for its own sake, then profits will follow.

Serving the deepest needs of people is the fundamental purpose of work. When we serve the deepest needs of others, we not only serve ourselves but also find meaning and purpose in our lives.

Kiehl's is a perfect example of an organization with a spiritual mission statement. The mission of Kiehl's was written over forty years ago by Aaron Morse, then president of Kiehl's, and sets the standards for and guiding philosophy of the company's products and customer service.

"A worthwhile firm must have a purpose for its existence. Not only the everyday work-a-day purpose to earn a just profit, but... to improve... the quality of the community to which it is committed. Each firm—as should each person—contributes to those around it...."

At our core, all of us are spiritual beings. And the essence of spirituality is wholeness. When we are whole, we are connected not only to every part of ourselves but also to the entire universe.

Fred Rogers wasn't spiritual because he was a minister. He became a minister because he was spiritual.

> A ministry doesn't have to be only through a church, or even through an ordination. And I think we all can minister to others in this world by being compassionate and caring. I hope you will feel good enough about yourselves that you will want to minister to others, and that you will find your own unique ways to do that.
>
> —Fred Rogers

Spirituality: The Constant Search for Meaning and Purpose

Most people that Ian interviewed had no trouble in saying what spirituality meant to them. To summarize: *Spirituality is both the intense feeling of being totally integrated as a person, and it's the feeling of being totally connected with the entire universe. Spirituality is the fundamental basis for ultimate meaning, purpose, and responsibility in people's lives.*

Ian found that people want to bring their whole person, or the complete package, to work. People report that they are frustrated with having to leave significant parts of themselves at home when they report for work. The search for wholeness is a critical component in the constant quest for meaning and purpose in one's life.

When Ian asked people how much of themselves they can bring to work, they reported that they can mainly bring only their brains, but not their deepest feelings and emotions, let alone their souls. Many organizations foster the illusion that one can split off and isolate reason from feelings and emotions. This illusion is one of the major indignities that people suffer at the hands of organizations. They are forced to split the cognitive or thinking parts of themselves apart from the emotional, ethical, and spiritual.[3]

This has the dire consequence that organizations do not reap the full creativity of their employees, and employees do not get the opportunity to develop themselves as whole human beings. Their work does not contribute to a sense of who they are and what they are. In turn, this means that employees cannot relate fully to one another, and hence, even less so to their customers.

Concluding Remarks: The Meaning of Enthusiasm

The roots of the word "enthusiasm" are "ens" and "theos." "Ens" means within and "theos" means spirit or God. Enthusiasm is literally the "spirit or the God within."

How can anything significant be accomplished without enthusiasm? How could one ever hope to find meaning and purpose in one's life without enthusiasm?

Whether we know it or not, every time an organization asks its employees to be enthusiastic, it is asking them to be spiritual.

Fred Rogers was the epitome of enthusiasm. His life had meaning and purpose because he helped others to find it in their lives as well. This was his purpose.

CHAPTER 14

Daniel Tiger and the Snowstorm

The story of Daniel Tiger is about the importance of being connected with other people. Through our connections with others, we are able to do and to be things that we cannot by ourselves. While we know this to be true for young children, it is no less true for adults. And it is certainly true of the child that is still in each of us.

Let's look at the story through the adult lens of the workplace. The snow is a metaphor for those times when we are overwhelmed with too much to do. The fact that the snow in the story is cereal suggests that the tasks that are overwhelming us may be mundane, as mundane as cereal, but they are still more than we can handle. (At a deeper level, it is about societies like ours that are relatively still so affluent that they are literally drowning in their own abundance—in this case, food—while many people around the world are dying from the lack of food. Sadly, as we write, the number of poor and impoverished in our own society has increased dramatically.)

Many of us react just as Daniel did in such a situation—we retreat to a safe place and hope that the problems will just go away. Some of us react the way that King Friday did, that is, by seeking fancy tools to apply to the task, for example, cereal-proof armor and blankets, and/or commanding the job to be done. Both Daniel's approach (running away from the problem) and King Friday's approach (bringing in fancy tools, i.e., technology, and invoking authority) represent extreme ways of dealing with the situation. Neither of these approaches worked. Only those colleagues who observed what was happening and were capable of working together were able to formulate a creative and practical solution that actually solved the problem.

The first step was to pay complete attention to their colleague and to understand what the real underlying fear was that kept him from solving the problem (Daniel was afraid he would drown) and then employ a low-tech, creative tool that dealt with the specific issue at hand (the inflatable boat). The second step was to offer help and support to the colleague until he or she regained control of the situation (the snowing stopped).

The story of Daniel and the Snowstorm is a metaphor for connectedness. When we are connected with others, we are connected with the deepest parts of ourselves. Or, in the words of Fred Rogers, "We speak with more than our mouths. We listen with more than our ears."

Connectedness is speaking and listening with our whole being, our whole person. It is speaking and listening—mostly listening—so that we can truly hear another person. It is putting our needs aside so that we can attend to the needs of others. It is listening without judging. It is listening with our heads, our hearts, and most of all, our souls. It is hearing the spirit of another.

We Are All Hard Wired to Connect

Humans have a deep need to connect with others. We are physically hard-wired by Nature to connect with others.

Research in the neurosciences demonstrates that our brains—our entire nervous systems—are hard-wired to experience the emotions that others are feeling. For instance, if another person exhibits anger, happiness, or sadness, then those parts of our brains that experience those same emotions are triggered within us. We feel the very same emotions that the other person is feeling and displaying, albeit to a lesser or a greater degree than the person initially experiencing them. The story of Daniel Tiger and the Snowstorm illustrates this well. Lady Aberlin and Neighbor Aber feel Daniel's fear, and because they share it, they help him overcome it.

Think of it this way. Our nervous systems are like telephone receivers (or in today's world, smart phones) that are always off the hook. They are always listening (or texting) for others ready to start a conversation. However, only when we care do we consciously attend to a particular person, or connection, at the other end of the line. That is, because our bodies and minds are hard-wired to connect *automatically* does not mean that we necessarily *care* about or listen to every possible connection with equal attentiveness. It merely means that our bodies and our minds don't have to think about connecting to others. Nature does this for us automatically. However, what we do with a particular connection depends on how we feel—care—about it.

There is another critical aspect of connectedness that comes from the writings and philosophy of Fred. It is articulated in the following quote from Fred and in the story "Good Friends":

> Anything that's human is mentionable, and anything that is mentionable can be more manageable. When we can talk about our feelings, they become less overwhelming, less upsetting, and less scary. The people we trust with that important talk can help us know that we're not alone.

Read carefully the comments of a high-ranking military officer that Friedman and Mandelbaum talked to in their book *That Used to Be Us*:

> Collaboration is important on the battle field and trust is the cement of collaboration.... And trust is the prerequisite for creativity. You will never be creative if you think that what you have to say will be discounted. So creativity cannot happen without trust, communication cannot happen without trust, and collaboration cannot happen without trust. It is the essential driver....[1]

CHAPTER 15

Concluding Remarks on Leadership

The overarching principle of this book is that there is a desperate need to create healthier organizations: organizations that promote the *emotional health* of their members. We not only deserve Planet Prism organizations but also have a fundamental human right to expect and to demand them.

To achieve the goal of healthier organizations, we need to revise our basic concepts of leadership. Most books on leadership that are found in bookstores or airports and read during a flight across the country are built around the idea of quick fixes, one version or another of "the ten things that you need to do to become a leader." (In this regard, the Seven C's in this book are not things, but fundamental human processes that one works on and hopefully improves over the entire course of one's life.) Many of them are based on the metaphor of climbing the corporate ladder, or of rising to the top.

An example is the book by Harold J. Leavitt entitled *Top Down: Why Hierarchies Are Here to Stay and How to Manage Them More Effectively*.[1]

Leavitt is quite clear about what hierarchies breed. He cites "infantilizing dependency that generates distrust, conflict, toadying, territoriality, backstabbing, distorted communication, and most of the other ailments that plague every large organization." Nevertheless, Leavitt makes the case that we will continue to develop hierarchies because hierarchies are efficient. In effect, we are stuck with them.

Hierarchical organizations are antithetical to the notion of organizations as neighborhoods, that is, where everyone is a member and not just nameless and faceless employees. The entire philosophy of this book is that it does not have to be this way, that it is possible for us to change to a new model of leadership that will allow, even encourage, greater emotional health among all workers.

This new vision of leadership is summed up in five simple principles, and each principle is further defined through quotes from Fred Rogers. The new vision of leadership begins with principle number one—the recognition that who we are and how we act as leaders has a profound effect on those around us.

> Principle #1: Everyone is a leader no matter where he or she is in an organization.
>
> If you could only sense how important you are to the lives of those you meet, how important you can be to the people you may never even dream of. There is something of yourself that you leave at every meeting with another person.
>
> —Fred Rogers

This statement does not say if you, the CEO, could only sense how important you are to the lives of those you meet. Rather, "you" refers to everyone, at any place and in any role within an organization. When we acknowledge that we are the sum total of all the experiences we've had growing up and coming to adulthood, and that we bring all of those stories with us to our adult role in the workplace, we are acknowledging that we are all leaders who are leading at some time every day of our lives. This is true whether we are a CEO, acting as the head of a department, helping a co-worker solve a problem, coaching a soccer game with our children, or planning an offsite workshop with our colleague. Wherever we are in an organization, we have a leadership role to perform at some point every day of our lives. Internalizing this idea is more empowering than we realize.

> Think of the ripple effect that can be created when we nourish someone. One kind empathetic word has a wonderful way of turning into many.
>
> —Fred Rogers

> Principle #2: Lifelong self-discovery is a basic requirement of leadership.

> Discovering the truth about ourselves is the work of a lifetime, but it's worth the effort.
>
> —Fred Rogers

True leadership is built upon the concept of discovering "who I am," of staying open to building self-awareness across the course of an entire life. Warren Bennis is one of the few contemporary writers on leadership who understands that quick fixes won't work. On the subject of self-discovery, Bennis says, "People begin to become leaders at that moment when they decide for themselves how to be." Bennis's interviews with leaders from all walks of life showed that the processes of self-knowledge and self-invention are necessary, sometimes painful, always personal, and never ending. The leaders he interviewed agreed to one thing: "No one can teach you how to become yourself, to take charge, to express yourself, except you."

> Principle #3: Love life and love what you do.
>
> The thing I remember best about successful people I've met through the years is their obvious delight in what they're doing . . . and it seems to have very little to do with worldly success. They just love what they're doing, and they love it in front of others.
>
> —Fred Rogers

It is equally important that a leader help others find the internal switch that will give them the opportunity to experience pleasure and self-fulfillment in their work. Fred found the inner switch within himself when he brought together his interests in music, story, child development, and technology to create his television program. His guiding principle was to use music, storytelling, child development, and television technology to help the children in the viewing audience understand their feelings about themselves. But, in so doing, he was expressing his own passion, his own commitment. Fred Rogers said, "How children feel about themselves *is* what I care about most."

Leadership has to do with how we treat people: the people we are leading, the people we are following, the shift we have in our roles as leaders or followers, and the importance that we follow a few guiding principles.

> Principle #4: Communication is at the heart of leadership.

Recall the fable of Daniel the Tiger as Ring-Bearer:

Daniel was asked to be the ring-bearer at a wedding in Make-Believe. He was terrified at the thought of it. Some of his friends thought it may be because he was worried he couldn't do the job well, that maybe the ring would fall off the pillow, so they taped it on. But even that didn't help. His friends encouraged him to ask questions about the role of a ring-bearer and he asked if he'd have to wear a bear suit (isn't that what a "ring bear" would wear?)—as a timid tiger, he was afraid of bears—even of dressing up as one.

> Listening and trying to understand the needs of those we would communicate with seems to me to be the essential pre-requisite of any real communication. And we might as well aim for *real* communication.
> —Fred Rogers

It goes without saying that communication is a fundamental skill for leadership. In fact, leadership *is* communication. But *real* communication is the true goal and essence of leadership. In real communication, the leader conveys acceptance and respect for what a colleague is expressing. Real communication requires the practice of active listening—the opposite of passive listening. When one listens actively, one puts aside his or her own thoughts and viewpoints and strives for empathy with what the speaker is expressing and feeling. Active listening is a skill that can be learned and one that must be practiced. It is a skill that a true leader must have.

> We speak with more than our mouths. We listen with more than our ears.
> —Fred Rogers

Principle #5: To gain power, give it away.

> *Put real value into play as part of work*: "One of the greatest paradoxes about omnipotence is that we need to feel it early in life, and lose it early in life, in order to achieve a healthy, realistic, yet exciting, sense of potency later on."
> —Fred Rogers

Contrary to many of our common notions, leadership does not mean omnipotence. The boss who feels omnipotent toward underlings has not resolved an important phase of development.

Beginning around the age of two years, the child begins to realize his or her separateness from his or her parents. That realization is both frightening and empowering, and it is fundamental to the development of a sense of self. It is a time of necessarily intense self-love that is ultimately tempered by the need to be loved by others. These conflicts are usually resolved by adolescence, but if they are not resolved, self-love sometimes wins out and the person can only feel secure by feeling superior to, or having power over, others.

True leadership is not the exercise of power. In fact, the terms *leadership* and *power* are antithetical to each other. True leadership is the ability to give power to others.

> Almost anything that extends our children's control over the world around them is bound to have a strong lure for them. In itself, that urge is a tremendous motivation for creativity and invention, for learning how to control disease or for finding ways to make deserts bloom.
>
> —Fred Rogers

The statement is equally true for adults in the workplace. Extending a co-worker's control over his or her job will inspire the development of new and novel ways for solving problems. *A leader is someone who gives away power, not hoards it for himself or herself.*

Concluding Remarks

We are well aware that many books on leadership already exist. As we read them, time and time again, we have been struck by the following words from Fred. We hope that they serve to inspire the development of your own personal leadership:

> I recently learned that in an average lifetime a person walks about sixty-five thousand miles. That's two and a half times around the world. I wonder where your steps will take you. I wonder how you'll use the rest of the miles you're given.
>
> —Fred Rogers

Hundreds of years ago the Jesuits articulated a model of leadership. It is consistent with the one espoused by Fred Rogers.

Four basic principles underlie the Jesuit model of leadership and that of Fred:

- We are all leaders and we are all leading all the time, well or poorly.
- Leadership springs from within. It's about who I am as much as what I do.
- Leadership is not an act. It is my life, a way of living.
- I never complete the task of becoming a leader; it's an on-going process.[2]

As we said before, no one is right for every organization, and no organization is right for every person. But everyone has an organization, a neighborhood that is right for him or her.

If we had to summarize thus far the entire thrust of this book, it would be as follows:

> The true measure of every organization is whether its healthiest members rise to the top, and not just those who are the smartest, the most political, the savviest, or the most cunning.

PART III

Putting the Seven Cs to Work

CHAPTER 16

Specialized Topics

In this section of the book, we introduce and use some specialized topics that are important to understand how and why organizations function. They are important because they give us a deeper understanding of individuals and organizations.

At the outset, we need to make very clear that the particular topics that we've chosen are ours alone. The topics do not represent the ideas of Fred Rogers. In fact, they are not intended to represent them. Nonetheless, we believe that they strongly complement Fred's ideas. Indeed, they help us better understand Fred's ideas especially as they pertain to the workplace.

We have selected six topics that provide theoretical underpinnings to the lessons that result from our analysis of the fables. We've also selected these particular six topics because we believe that they are not given the degree of attention they deserve in business schools curricula, in the academic literature on business, and in programs of organizational behavior. This is especially true of our interpretation, applications, and the practical techniques that our colleagues and we have discovered that can be used to implement the topics in group and organizational settings. But most of all, they provide deeper insight into the fables, and the Seven Cs as well.

Above all, we have selected the particular topics because they speak directly to the never-ending need to better understand ourselves, others, and the innumerable interactions that occur between individuals and groups. This is especially the case if we are to develop leadership for healthy organizations.

The particular topics we explore in greater detail and how each of them contributes to the necessary skills for leadership are as follows: Life Skills, Conflict Management Styles, Defense Mechanisms, Personality Styles and Types, Crisis Management, and Attachment Theory. We not only present the topics in this order, but also show how each gives a better understanding of your own decisions and behavior and the behavior of others, and how individual styles and decision-making behavior impact group dynamics.

We have also developed specific exercises that the instructor should conduct *before* the students read about the theory behind a particular topic area. The exercises are intended to maximize each student's understanding of the topics. The exercises are found in the EXERCISE section at the end of the book.

We recommend strongly that each of the following sections not be read until after the instructor has carried out the experiential exercise associated with a particular topic and discussed it thoroughly with the class.

Special Topics

(To the instructor: Please see Exercise #1)

Life Skills

Research has identified seven essential skills that enable us to manage our attention, emotions, and behavior to attain one's goals.[1] One cannot practice effective leadership without one's awareness of and the ability to call upon each of these seven essential life skills. They are as follows: (1) focus and self-control, (2) perspective-taking, (3) communicating, (4) making connections, (5) critical thinking, (6) taking on challenges, and (7) self-directed, engaged learning. To be sure, all of these are intellectual skills in the sense that they have strong cognitive components. But they are much more than this. They involve weaving together social, emotional, and intellectual capacities and capabilities.

Studies reveal that the boundaries between the cognitive and social emotional regions and mechanisms of the brain are in fact extremely fluid. Indeed, different parts of the brain work together when we are engaged in action or learning. Kurt Fischer, a brain researcher at Harvard says:

> One of the most beneficial things that brain research has done is it's made it very hard for us to split cognition from emotion. For example, the areas of the brain most involved in memory—the quintessential cognitive function—are strongly tied to the emotion areas.
>
> (see Galinsky 2010, p. 322)

The research on which the seven essential life skills are based is described in *Mind in the Making: The Seven Essential Life Skills Every Child Needs* (2010) by Ellen Galinsky. Galinsky spent ten years interviewing and filming prominent researchers on children. She also reviewed thousands of studies about human growth and development.

While Galinsky's work primarily focuses on research on child development, the findings are applicable across the entire life span. Galinsky is the president of the Families and Work Institute. As a consequence, she is extremely well aware of the skills needed for success in the workplace of the twenty-first century. She points out that the skills "are not only important for children; we as adults need them just as much as children do." They are life skills that involve the *executive functions* of the brain. Maybe you learned them when you were a child. Maybe you didn't, but you won't be sure until you take stock of your own ability to recognize and access these skills, which reside in the prefrontal cortex of the brain and you do so with the knowledge that it is never too late to learn or improve upon them.

The following is a brief description of the seven essential life skills.

Skill #1, Focus and self-control: It goes without saying that we live and work in a complex, fast-moving, exciting, and stressful world. The ability to determine what is important and pay attention to this amid distractions requires focus and self-control. The executive functions involved in accomplishing focus and self-control include paying attention, remembering necessary rules, and inhibiting one's initial response to achieve a larger goal.

One of the classic studies about focus and self-control is known as the Marshmallow Test. In this particular study, children are given a choice between one marshmallow right now or more than one marshmallow later. Some children could wait to get more than one marshmallow later and some couldn't. Those who could wait, that is, endure delaying the gratification of getting the treat, "were more likely to do better in many ways as they grew up, including pursuing their academic and personal goals with less frustration and distraction"(see Galinsky 2010, p. 5).

Think of the marshmallow as a metaphor for your own ability to wait and to delay gratification in order to achieve a larger goal. Haven't there been times when you wanted something more, but you couldn't wait and so you settled for just one marshmallow?

This skill requires more than just sticking to a task to the point of where one develops tunnel vision, for example, disregarding valuable, new input. The skill also requires *cognitive flexibility*, the ability to adjust and change as new priorities emerge, and the use of *working memory*, the ability to tap information stored in the brain and update it or relate it to new information. The components of focus and self-control can be developed and enhanced at any age.

Skill #2, Perspective-taking: This skill refers to the ability to step outside of yourself and figure out what others think and feel. In her book *The Outside-in Corporation*,[2] Barbara Bund cites eminent management scholar Peter Drucker's description of the "outside-in perspective—seeing things as a customer would see them." As Drucker described it, this requires a shift from an inside-out perspective ("You take what we make") to an outside-in perspective. ("We seek to understand your problems and will surprise you by solving them.") This description does not, however, do justice to the developmental importance of the skill or its significance in relationship building, work success, and life success in general. Galinsky describes perspective-taking as an essential skill for thriving. It is truly a social-emotional-intellectual skill.

To exercise perspective-taking, we need to call upon specific executive functions of the brain: *inhibitory control* of our own thoughts and feelings to consider the thoughts and feelings of others; *cognitive flexibility*, which allows us to shift from one point of view to another;

and *reflection* as we compare and contrast another's point of view to our own. Understanding and articulating what is going on in the mind of another person builds metalinguistic ability, the ability to reflect on the **use** of language, the ability to recognize that language has both literal and implied meaning. We don't typically or consciously teach children or adults how to take the perspective of others, but it can be taught. Teaching and practicing taking on the perspective of others has many advantages, including one that is particularly important to our ability to manage in the workplace, that is, the ability to handle conflict and aggression.

Research has shown that children who have been helped to understand, to take the perspective of others, have less of a need to strike back when conflicts erupt. Some youngsters and some adults have a "hostile attribution bias," which leads them to assume that any infraction suggests hostility, and this leads to conflict. With help, those who hold a hostile attribution bias can learn to take a different perspective on a given situation, not jump to conclusions about the intentions of others, and take the time to consider other problem-solving skills in place of aggression (see Galinsky 2010, pp. 85–87). As we will see when we use perspective-taking to analyze the fables, those encounters in which one stops to look at the situation from the perspective of another have more positive outcomes.

Skill #3, Communication: All of us are born with the innate ability and the need to communicate. As we grow and develop, we use language, both verbal and written, to share our thoughts and experiences with others. Communication is more than just saying what we want to say in a way that will be understood by others. It is also about listening and hearing the communication from others. To repeat a quote from Fred, "We speak with more than our mouths. We listen with more than our ears." Communication is the complex interplay of language, gesture, intent, personality, and even context.

Obviously, we communicate all the time. Or more accurately, we talk all of the time. But talking and communicating are definitively not the same thing. And yet survey after survey of the skills that employers look for, skills that are used in every position, in every industry, and on every job, finds that verbal and written communication skills are considered to be most important. At the same time, other surveys find that employers report that the biggest gaps in the skills of new employees are in the areas of spoken and written communication. Why do these gaps exist and what can we, as leaders, do to close the gaps? The first step is a clear recognition of the problem, and the willingness to confront it.

Skill #4, Making connections: Our society is going through a profound and fundamental transformation from an industrial society to a knowledge society. In a knowledge society, information is so readily available that there is little to be gained by filling our heads with facts because we can easily get what we need when we need it. It is all the more essential to cultivate in employees and ourselves the ability to make creative, interesting, unique, and useful connections with information. As Adele Diamond of the University of British Columbia put it, "The essence of creativity is to be able to disassemble and recombine elements in new ways" (see Galinsky 2010, p. 182). The ability to make connections, to think creatively, is another of the skills that employers find lacking in candidates.

Wayne C. Johnson, Hewlett Packard's vice president of University Relations Worldwide, says that too often, college graduates come into HP with technical knowledge, "but what is missing is using the right side of the brain—where communication and creativity takes place." Making connections, thinking creatively, calls upon these functions: working memory, inhibitory control, and cognitive flexibility. But how do we help people tap these functions in ways that result in creative thinking? One tested way is through the arts. Participation in the arts teaches us how to think. Galinsky (p. 186) cites a researcher who explains why the arts are so important: "The arts may have survival value in enabling us to reach beyond ourselves to imagine, to understand metaphor, and perhaps to prepare for the unknown."

Skill #5, Critical thinking: Critical thinking is another skill that calls upon metacognition: critical thinking requires that we think about thinking by reflecting, analyzing, reasoning, planning, and evaluating (see Galinsky 2010, p. 204). Critical thinking requires that we search for the kind of knowledge that we can show to be valid and reliable so that it can guide our beliefs, decisions, and actions. It short, it demands the ability to be self-aware and self-critical about our fundamental assumptions. It also requires the ability to understand how our assumptions influence the conclusions we reach, the decisions we make, and the actions we take.

How can we help ourselves and employees know whether there are more questions to be asked, whether the information we've selected is trustworthy and reliable? One of the ways we do this is by knowing to whom we can turn for accurate, trustworthy information. We need to do this because from the time we are born through adulthood, we are incredibly dependent on knowledge that resides in the minds of others. The need for a reliable brain trust begins early in life.

Children progress through distinct developmental stages with regard to their ability to seek and trust the knowledge and information provided by others. The stages include figuring out who will be helpful and cooperative rather than off-putting, recognizing when help is needed, and differentiating between sources of accurate information versus inaccurate or biased information. We engage in the same processes as adults. It is clear that critical thinking includes using interpersonal skills to understand the intentions of others.

An additional stage that warrants discussion is the role of curiosity. Recent research with children has shown that one of the things that provoke curiosity is encountering something that violates prior beliefs. When this happens, one either denies the evidence, tries to explain it away, or accepts that a prior belief is wrong and has to change, which leads to the need for more information. One's curiosity is thereby engaged. Curiosity is an important component of critical thinking, but even more important is the role of engagement.

Critical thinking is not merely a sequence of dry intellectual processes. It often involves both "hot" and "cold" situations, for example, relatively abstract situations that we don't care much about (cold) in contrast to deeply personal situations where we have a stake in the consequences (hot). In the latter instances, emotions play a great part in the processes we use. We cannot and should not seek to remove emotion from the decisions we make, but instead recognize the role that they play and learn when it helps to take a step back, for example, create psychological distance, to gain a new perspective.

Skill #6, Taking on challenges: We have an innate need to be able to take on new challenges rather than avoid or simply cope with them. We also want employees to be open to new challenges. But new challenges are often stressful. The challenges of working and competing in the "knowledge society" coupled with the increasing pace of everyday living can be stressful. Megan Gunnar, director of the Institute of Child Development at the University of Minnesota, defines stress as "when demands on your body or your expectations of those demands exceed your ability to handle them" (see Galinsky 2010, p. 250). Stress has a specific effect on the body's physiology. The effects are so automatic that one cannot control them. Understanding this has implications for your role as a leader. If you know or suspect that an employee is under stress, whether from something going on in their outside life or within the workplace, it is an opportunity to be helpful to that person. Indeed, we would say that an ethical leader has a responsibility to help that person.

A supportive environment is obviously important. Acknowledging, not denying, stress is an important step. Additionally, helping someone take control of stress often occurs by breaking things down into small, manageable pieces.

Another finding from developmental research that has implications for leaders comes from the *theory of mindsets*. The theory holds that there are two fundamentally different *mindsets* that people hold about their capabilities: a *fixed versus a growth mindset*.

Those with a fixed mindset believe that their intelligence is an unchangeable trait such that when they meet a new challenge that they can't handle, they conclude that they are just not smart enough. As a result, they give up sooner. Those with a growth mindset believe that intelligence can be improved and increased by things like new strategies and more practice. As a result, they keep trying and don't give up.

Researchers have explored how such mindsets came into being and whether they could be changed or not. They have found that those who were praised only for intelligence ("you're so smart"; "you must be really smart") tended to give up as tasks became more difficult. In contrast, those who were praised for effort ("you must have worked really hard"; "you used some interesting strategies") kept going as the level of difficulty of the challenge increased. There's s lot to be learned from these findings about motivating people to take on new challenges.

Skill #7, Self-directed, engaged learning: One of the most important things we can do for ourselves, for the people we supervise, for the organizations we work for, for the world we wish to create is to facilitate life-long learning. When we exercise the essential skills outlined earlier in this chapter, everything comes together to make one into a self-directed, engaged learner. Implementing a few principles helps to realize this goal:

(1) Acknowledge that we need to integrate all the various modalities by which we learn: We cannot overemphasize that there is no real separation in the mind and body between social, emotional, and cognitive learning. We would also add that there is no separation between social, emotional, cognitive, physical, and kinesthetic learning as well. The latter, physical and kinesthetic learning, are developed by engaging in music, art, and sports. The general principle is, therefore, to help employees find something they deeply care about and facilitate their pursuit of it.

(2) Elaborate and extend: When we help young children elaborate and reflect upon their experiences, they not only build their communication skills but also gain a deeper understanding of them. The same is true of adults. But, even more fundamental, the process of learning itself needs to be challenged. The process in turn that does this is referred to as stretch assignments, meaning assignments that push us beyond what we think we can do. Assignments such as these are important for learning and for motivation. However, be very mindful of and watch for unproductive stress that they can easily cause. This comes from being stretched too far, too fast.

(3) Practice, synthesize, and generalize: Provide opportunities for people to explain what they've learned.

(4) Help people to become increasingly accountable: Recall Fred's comments about rules, "Rules are a gift we give to our children." This is also true of accountability. Provide people with the space to make mistakes and to learn from them.
(5) Create a community of learners: James Heckman, a Nobel Prize winner and professor at the University of Chicago said, "Motivation begets motivation" (see Galinsky 2010, p. 11). To paraphrase Heckman, leaders foster motivation in employees by being motivated themselves. This is the first step toward becoming a learning organization. Unless you yourself are motivated and excited about life-long learning, you can't create a culture that encourages and supports continuous employee learning, critical thinking, and risk taking with new ideas; allows mistakes; and values employee contributions.

(To the instructor: Please see the Life Skills exercise)

Conflict Management Styles

Conflict is an inevitable aspect of life. Accordingly, people react differently to it. Kenneth W. Thomas and Ralph H. Kilmann developed an important and powerful framework as well as an instrument, the Thomas-Kilmann Conflict Mode Instrument (TKI), for measuring a person's conflict-handling style.

The framework has two dimensions: (1) how much a person expects or strives to *get* from another person out of a conflict situation and (2) how much a person expects or strives to *give* to another.

Imagine a pie. If one avoids conflict at any cost, then one never gets a piece of a pie, indeed, any pie. This style is called an Avoider.

If one always takes the whole pie and never gives away any piece of it, then one is Competitive. If one always gives away one's share of the pie, then one an Accommodator.

If one is willing to settle for half of the pie, then one is a Compromiser. If one works to increase the size of the pie so that everyone can have a whole pie, then one is a Collaborator.

The ideal is to have all of these various styles in one's psychological repertoire so that one can call on them when the situation demands it. Where the stakes are not high—the situation is not important—avoiding conflict often is the best choice. When the stakes are high—such as getting out of a burning building and there is no time to collaborate or debate who is right—a competitive style works best. When giving in to someone so that social harmony is preserved, accommodating is often best. Indeed, without any accommodation at all, society would not be possible. When one cannot get all of what one wants, but it is important for both parties to get something, then compromise is called for. And when there is time to get to know and trust one's opponents, convert them into allies, and work together, collaboration is best.

There is a simple mathematical equation that describes these various styles: The amount of the pie one *gets* plus the amount one *gives* equals the size of the pie (the amount or number of pies). That is, $Get + Give = Size$. For avoiders, $Get = Give = 0$. In this case, $Give + Get = 0$. That is, neither party gets anything. For competitors, $Get = 1$ and $Give = 0$. Thus, $Give + Get = 1$ (one pie). For accommodators, $Get = 0$ and $Give = 1$. Once again, $Give + Get = 1$. For compromisers, $Get = Give = 0.5$. Therefore, $Give + Get = 1$. And for collaborators, $Get = Give = 1$, which means, $Give + Get = 2$.

The TKI helps groups and individuals recognize and process the strong feelings of fear, anger, and frustration that are part of conflict and move toward constructive outcomes. The Thomas-Kilmann framework helps us discover that conflict-handling styles are not absolutely right or wrong. They are merely different. Understanding and recognizing different styles of handling conflict and knowing one's preferred style helps us to alter, adapt, and ideally select a style that is better suited to a particular situation.

To summarize, the different modes for handling conflict are as follows:

Competing: high assertiveness and low cooperativeness—the goal is to win.
Avoiding: low assertiveness and low cooperativeness—the goal is to delay or to stop something completely.
Compromising: moderate assertiveness and moderate cooperativeness—the goal is to find a middle ground.

Collaborating: high assertiveness and high cooperativeness—the goal is to find a win-win solution.
Accommodating: low assertiveness and high cooperativeness—the goal is to yield.

As you develop the ability to recognize these different styles in yourself and others, hopefully you'll find that this knowledge gives you the insight and skills to manage critical problems such as the following:

- Change and the conflicts that change elicits;
- Communication, especially when conflict erupts;
- Developing your own leadership skills and those of others;
- Increasing employee satisfaction and retention;
- Improving performance and performance evaluations;
- Understanding and managing stress;
- Improving team-building skills;
- Managing and improving negotiation skills.

(To the instructor: Please see Exercise #3)

Defense Mechanisms

If Sigmund Freud had discovered nothing more than defense mechanisms, it would have been more than enough to ensure his lasting fame.

On occasion, everyone uses various defense mechanisms to protect oneself from disturbing, unpleasant ideas and messages. The range of defense mechanisms is broad. It includes denial, compartmentalization, idealization, splitting, projection, and projective identification.

If an event or a situation is highly disturbing or unpalatable such as directly witnessing the death of a loved one, becoming a victim of incest or a serious crime, or witnessing the horrors of war, one's mind can literally shut down and refuse to register the event, or at least to do so consciously. This is an example of outright *denial*. But since denial is never perfect, unpleasant experiences often resurface in the form of dreams, nightmares, and severe anxiety attacks in response to, say, loud noises that are mistaken for gunshots.

Compartmentalization occurs when one part of the mind registers one part of a horrific event—say, the sounds—and others register the sights and smells associated with it. But since it would be too overwhelming, and hence traumatic, if the sights, sounds, and smells were brought together as parts of a single experience, the mind unconsciously keeps them apart.

Projection occurs when we disown parts of ourselves that we don't like and project them onto others. *Projective identification* occurs when we accept or identify with—"own"—the projections of others.

For instance, a few years ago, Ian asked people to describe the times in their lives when they had been betrayed: Who betrayed them? What happened and why they thought it occurred? Most importantly, he asked: How would you compare yourself in relation to those who betrayed you.

Two highly distinct and disturbing portraits emerged. Those who had been betrayed described themselves in extremely glowing terms. They were warm, trusting, highly ethical, and outgoing. In contrast, those who had betrayed them were described in completely opposite and highly negative terms. They were cold-blooded, completely untrustworthy, unethical, and withdrawn. That is, we often project onto others that which we don't like, and therefore, don't acknowledge about ourselves.

In short, we both demonize those who have betrayed us and we loathe them.[3] The psychological mechanism that underlies this basic phenomenon is known as *splitting*.[4] From time to time, all of us divide, or split, the world into good guys versus bad guys. We project all the things we don't like about others and ourselves onto the bad guys and we take into ourselves (*introject*) all the highly idealized qualities we like about ourselves—the proverbial good guys.

Unless splitting is seen for what it is—an all-too-common mechanism that helps us to cope with disappointment and loss—an organization, person, or society cannot honestly face up to, let alone solve, its problems. Indeed, those organizations, persons, and societies will only continue to blame their problems on others with the result that others will retaliate, dishing out more of the same. Projections and counter-projections will fly back and forth. Over time, they will intensify to the point that they suck up all the energy of the person or organization. In extreme cases, people strike back by engaging in verbal and physical acts of abuse and even sabotage. When this happens, the organization has degenerated to the point that it has become deeply pathological.

Defense mechanisms per se are not inherently bad. Indeed, Nature put them in us at the very beginning of life for a very special reason. The world is too complex and confusing for young children to take all of it in without being hopelessly overwhelmed. Therefore, in the beginning, the full complexity of reality has to be denied. Obviously, this process does not begin and end during childhood. It continues through our entire adult lives. The positive side of defense mechanisms is that they can help to

1. Minimize anxiety;
2. Protect a fragile ego;
3. Maintain repression, that is, the unconscious process by which the mind refuses to acknowledge painful and unacceptable events, and so on.

In turn, repression

1. Prevents discomfort;
2. Leads to some economy of time and effort by not having to deal fully with complex situations.

Nonetheless, the goal of understanding defense mechanisms is to recognize when one or another type of mechanism is being used and to determine whether or not it is healthy for the particular situation or individual. Obviously, the complete denial of reality is not helpful.

(To the instructor: please see Exercise #4)

Personality Styles and Types

Organizations are made up of many different kinds of people having many different types of personalities. In particular, the work of the Swiss psychoanalyst/psychiatrist Carl Jung provides special insight into how personalities differ, how they impact individual and group behavior, problem-solving, teamwork, and competition. Jung was originally a close friend and collaborator of Sigmund

Freud; Jung and Freud parted company over their radically differing interpretations of psychoanalysis.

As was the case with most educated Europeans of his time, Jung (1875–1961) was especially well schooled in European art, history, literature, and philosophy, just to mention a few of the many subjects in which he was knowledgeable. In 1921, in his native language German, Jung published one of his most important books *Psychological Types*.[5] In it, Jung presented a framework of different personality types that he found repeatedly in European art, history, literature, philosophy, poetry, politics, science, and other aspects of culture. No matter what the particular field of knowledge or profession he looked at, Jung found the same underlying differences and how they manifested themselves in their approach to any issue or topic.

Later, Isabel Briggs Myers (1897–1980) and her mother, Katherine Briggs (1875–1968), took Jung's typology and developed the Myers-Briggs Type Indicator (a psychological inventory), which allowed one to measure a person's personality type. The instrument has been validated and used across many age and occupational groups to help people understand the different ways in which people take in information and make decisions about typical situations encountered in everyday life.

It is extremely important to note that there are no right or wrong answers to the items contained in the Myers-Briggs inventory. That is, it is not a measure of healthy versus unhealthy or pathological states of mind. All of the types are capable of health. Each is necessary depending upon the circumstances.

We abbreviate the Myers-Briggs Type Indicator as Myers-Briggs.

Sixteen Different Personality Types

According to the Myers-Briggs, there are sixteen different personality types. These arise by combining the polar opposites or ends of four underlying dimensions:

- Introvert/Extravert, or I versus E
- Sensing/Intuiting or S versus N
- Thinking/Feeling or T versus F
- Perceiving/Judging or P versus J

Combining the ends of the dimensions in all possible ways results in sixteen different combinations or personality types, e.g., ISTJ, ENFP, and so on. That is, two times two times two times two equals sixteen possible different combinations.

Introverts versus Extraverts

Although the terms *Introvert* and *Extravert* have entered into everyday language, what Jung meant by them is very different from common usage. We hear these misinterpretations of Jung's meanings in our work with students and executives all the time when we ask them for their definitions of these two terms. It is common to have Introverts defined as someone who is shy, withdrawn, and closed off. Conversely, it is common to have Extraverts defined as people who are brash, loud, pushy, "groupies." These popular descriptions do not do justice to what Jung meant when he described Introverts versus Extraverts.

By Introvert or "I," Jung meant that someone's fundamental life energy or force comes entirely from within. In the first and last resort, for an Introvert, the standard for whether something or someone makes sense—indeed, is right or wrong—comes from within. It doesn't matter if 99 percent of the population feels differently as long as an Introvert or "I" feels that something is true or false to him or her. In other words, Is are the sole standards for their beliefs. For example, if an Introvert feels that abortion is perfectly acceptable, then it doesn't matter what others think or feel about it.

In contrast, the life energy or force of Extraverts, or Es, comes from others. Extraverts, Es, get their energy just from being around others. And they are generally in sync with the opinions of others. If 99 percent of the population agreed or disagreed with something, then this had a substantial effect on the beliefs of Es.

This doesn't mean that Es don't have any beliefs of their own or that they are pushovers for the beliefs and opinions of others. It just means that in general, Es thrive on the energy of others such that they prefer to be with others than to be alone.

Similarly, this doesn't mean that Is couldn't be persuaded to change their minds, but that they didn't necessarily need others to form their own beliefs. And given a choice, they would rather be alone than be with others. Indeed, Is often feel exhausted by being around large crowds.

Of course, most people are a mixture of these two extremes. Nonetheless, the extremes do exist. Furthermore, for clarity, it is far easier to describe the extremes than the mixtures that are hard to see unless one first understands the opposite ends of each dimension. In the Myers-Briggs, the extremes are called "pure types."

Sensing versus Intuiting

The Sensing/Intuiting (S/N) dimension refers to one's automatic or natural way of gathering information and understanding the world. (Note that the letter N is used to stand for Intuiting to differentiate this dimension from I, which stands for Introvert.) Figure 16.1 shows some of the important differences between Sensing and Intuiting.

In general, Ss prefer focusing on details and facts over big patterns and the big picture, which is the province of Ns. Ss are *reality based* whereas Ns are *possibility based*. Ss live in the here-and-now while Ns live in the future. While only facts are real to Ss, hypotheticals are just as real—even more so—to Ns. "What ifs" and hypotheticals give

S/N: Sensing vs. Intuiting	
Sensing:	Intuiting:
Only Individual Facts Are Real	Only Whole Patterns Are Real
Numbers / Details	What Ifs / Hypotheticals
Present Facts / Value	Future Possibilities / Values
Certain	Uncertain
Closed / Structured	Open / Unstructured
Specific / Precise	Big Picture / Vague
Single Right Answer	Multiple Interpretations
Down-to-Earth / Practical	In-the-Sky / Futuristic / Inventive
Stays Within Accepted Boundaries	Opens Up New Territories
Dislikes Ambiguity	Embraces Ambiguity
Creative	**Creative**
Intelligent	**Intelligent**

Figure 16.1 S Versus N, Sensing Versus Intuition

Ns room for their imaginations to soar, whereas facts hem them in. In sharp contrast, facts and details give Ss the grounding they need to feel safe and secure. It is not surprising then, that Ss hate ambiguity and uncertainty, while Ns thrive on them.

It is not that one type is inherently right and the other is wrong, but that both need each other to keep them honest. Without any facts, one can easily get lost in fantasies of imagination—castles in the air—and without any intuition one becomes mundane and devoid of imagination. Without Intuiting, without first seeing the big picture, one can easily get trapped into solving the wrong problems. And, without Sensing, without details and facts, one avoids actually solving real problems.

As you read the descriptions, if you feel instinctively that one applies to you more or one makes more sense than another, then without actually taking the Myers-Briggs, you are in effect "typing" yourself.

A common stereotype is that only Ns are creative. For this reason, it is very important to point out Ss and Ns are equally creative. They are just creative in different ways. Ss are creative in using well-known, well-accepted ideas and technologies, and improving on them. Ns excel in inventing new ideas and technologies. Every society—every organization—needs both forms of creativity.

Thinking versus Feeling

The Thinking/Feeling (T/F) dimension refers to one's most natural way of forming judgments and making choices. Figure 16.2 shows some of the important differences between T and F. In Figure 16.2, we will use the terms *objective* and *subjective* to illustrate a difference between those who operate from a Thinking versus a Feeling dimension or perspective. But we wish to point out that neither of the types is perfectly objective or subjective because perfect objectivity/subjectivity is not obtainable by humans. So while T types may presume that they are objective in their judgments and F types may presume that they are subjective in their judgments, they are not.

T/F: Thinking vs. Feeling	
Thinking:	Feeling:
Logic	Personal Likes / Dislikes
General Formulas	Personal Feelings
General Universal	**Particular / Unique**
Object-Oriented	People-Oriented
Objective	Subjective
Cold	Warm
Math / Economics	Psych / Soc
All Situations	Individual Situations
Creative	**Creative**
COGNITIVE IQ	**EMOTIONAL IQ**
Ethical Rules / Legal	**Ethical / What Feels Right**

Figure 16.2 T Versus F, Thinking Versus Thinking

Thinking, or T, types are analytical and detached. Ts instinctively like to analyze every situation using some systematic and logical framework before reaching a decision. In doing so, they look for what's general and universal such that it applies to everyone and all situations. Given that they are generally unconcerned with feelings and with people, they are oftentimes perceived as cold and uncaring.

Feeling, or F, types are the complete opposite of Ts. They are personal, attached, and lean toward subjectivity. (Once again, all of the types have a strong subjective aspect given that a human subject is involved in all knowledge.) People and personal feelings in the form of likes and dislikes are everything for Fs. That is, Fs reach a decision in terms of their personal likes and dislikes and the impacts they have on people.

While Ts are concerned with what's general in every situation, Fs are concerned with what's unique and special. While Ts quickly hone in on impersonal analytically based analyses of every situation, Fs instinctively provide intensely personal descriptions and explanations of anything. Where Ts are often bothered by the conflict between ideas, Fs are bothered by the conflict between people.

As you read the summary description of the Thinking and Feeling dimensions in Figure 16.2, see if one or the other more naturally appeals to you.

Once again, it's not a question of right versus wrong, but of fundamental differences in how different types perceive the world and hence what they perceive as right and wrong.

Perceiving versus Judging

The Perceiving/Judging dimension refers to whether one prefers or is more comfortable with taking in information or with taking action. P types are more comfortable taking in information without reaching a decision or taking action. J types are just the opposite. They are oriented primarily to taking action even when it is based on little or no information. Depending upon one's Myers-Briggs type, one uses either Sensing or iNtuiting to perceive or take in information about the world and Thinking or Feeling to make judgments or take action with regard to the information one has taken in. The whole S/N dimension is the P (perceiving) dimension, and the whole T/F dimension is the J (judging) dimension.

Figure 16.3 shows some of the important differences between Perceiving and Judging.

P types never have enough data, whether of the form of Sensing or iNtuiting, to reach a decision or closure. If one is an S and a P, then there is always one more piece of data to collect before reaching a decision. If one is an N and a P, then there is always one more big idea or picture to consider. In sharp contrast, J types are quick

J / P: Judging vs. Perceiving	
Judging(Decision):	Perceiving (Data Input):
Quick to Reach a Decision	Slow to Reach a Decision
Quick to Closure	Slow to Closure
Close Off Options	Keep All Options Open
Narrow Alternatives / Options	Broaden Alternatives / Options
Focus	Expansive
Impatient	Patient
Decisive	Indecisive
Instantly	Never
As Quickly As Possible	Delay As Long As Possible
One Data Point	Never Enough Data

Figure 16.3 J Versus P, Judging Versus Perceiving

to reach a decision or closure. One data set (Sensing) or one vision (iNtuiting) is sufficient.

Four Combined Types

Figure 16.4 shows four major combinations of the Myers-Briggs dimensions that are particularly important. They are ST, NT, NF, and SF. For the time being, we leave aside I/E and P/J because for our purposes it is not necessary to describe sixteen different types.

STs are a combination of the attributes of Sensing and Thinking. No matter what the issue or problem, STs break it down into its individual components or parts. (This is the Sensing part.) For each of the parts, they then gather specific data or facts (Sensing again) so that they can understand (Thinking) the issue or problem, and hence, solve it. For STs, unless someone can break a problem down into its separate parts and gather objective data on it, one can't even state the problem precisely, let alone solve it.

STs are also grounded in the here and now. They are supreme realists. They believe in only what they can feel, touch, hear, see, and smell. In other words, they are highly practical.

Furthermore, STs believe that it is only by analyzing something in terms of accepted logic and science that one really understands something. This is the Thinking part of their personality.

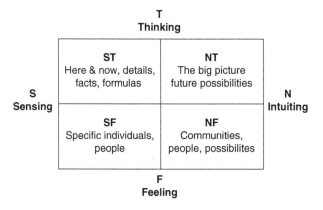

Figure 16.4   Four Combined Types

In contrast, NTs take a broad focus, if not the broadest possible view, of all issues and problems. They seek out the big picture. They believe in solving problems (this is their Thinking side) as well, but they don't believe in breaking problems down into their separate parts until they've looked at the whole system in which all problems reside. Unless they do this, they can't be sure that they are solving the right problems.

NTs excel at thinking outside of the box. They especially love new and novel ways of looking things. They are also idealists in that they believe their new ways of seeing things will make life better for everyone and therefore should be adopted as soon as possible. This is especially the case if one is an INTJ. INTJs believe that their own intuitive ideas are, of course, generally applicable.

NFs also look at the big picture and future possibilities. They are also idealists. But their focus is not on systems that are impersonal and abstract to them, but on whole communities of people. They are also concerned with the largest group of people imaginable—humankind.

Like STs, SFs are also concerned with details, but their sole focus is on specific individuals whom they know and with whom they live and work. Communities and notions like "humankind" are far too abstract and removed from the actual, concrete, living, breathing people to matter to them.

Notice that STs and NTs share at least one psychological function in common—Thinking. Likewise, NFs and SFs share Feeling. NTs and NFs share iNtuiting, and STs and SFs share Sensing. Therefore, STs and NTs can, if they wish, at least communicate through Thinking, and similarly for other types. But the diagonal types—ST and NF, and NT and SF—share nothing in common. They experience the greatest difficulty in communicating and understanding one another.

Fred Rogers did not make explicit use of the Jungian theory of personality types nor did he make reference to the Myers-Briggs for measuring preferences. However, as we will show, the characters from the Neighborhood of Make-Believe embody many of the characteristics described by Jung and in the terms of the Myers-Briggs. In fact, the characters are interesting and complex mixtures of the pure types. An interesting speculation is that these personality archetypes emerged in the characters that Fred Rogers created from the same collective unconscious source that Jung tapped when he analyzed art, history, literature, and the like to develop his theory of psychological types.

Group Problem Formulation

In Chapter 8, we referred to two methods by which helping groups look at their problems from very different standpoints to help ensure that they were solving the "right problem(s)." Recall that we put people at random into one of four groups. One group was asked to defend the status quo. Another was assigned to defend complete change. Two other groups were along the spectrum between no and complete change.

The Myers-Briggs gives a more general method for problem *formulation* by groups. That is, before one can solve a problem, one needs to know that one is working on the right problem to begin with. The Myers-Briggs helps to ensure that no matter the problem, there will be at least four very different formulations of it. In other words, while the Myers-Briggs may have started out in individual psychology, nothing prevents it from being used as a method of group problem solving, that is, social psychology.

If your current class or group is large enough to include a significant number of representatives from the other dimensions, for example, Introvert/Extravert and Perceiving/Judging, your instructor or leader may have you subdivide into groups where these dimensions are included in problem-solving exercises. Likewise, in your own organizations you might consider creating groups of like types in which the additional dimensions are represented in order to get the fullest possible range of problem formulation.

Is tend to focus on their own internal thoughts and feelings irrespective of the outside world. Es on the other hand focus their attention outward. A group of Js is always the first to finish an exercise, while Ps are still deciding up until the very last minute what problem to select and how to illustrate it.

The use of the Myers-Briggs for group problem solving is very different from what one typically gets in conventional business education. The Myers-Briggs shows how people view important problems very differently. Even more significantly, it also shows how those differences can be used constructively to produce multiple views of any problem. It also sets the stage for how various views can be integrated to produce holistic views of any problem. It certainly allows for a thoughtful discussion of the fact that in today's world none of the "pure" views can even pose, let alone fully solve our, complex problems. Integrating all of the views into a cohesive whole has become an absolute necessity. In other words, every problem has aspects that are Sensing Thinking, iNtuiting Thinking, Sensing Feeling, and iNtuiting Thinking. Unless, these are integrated, the use of any one of them without the others only makes things worse because we are then leaving out essential parts of the problem.

The Kidney Machine Problem

The Kidney Machine Problem is another important exercise. We normally use it after people have completed the first exercise and have been introduced to the Myers-Briggs. This exercise really brings home the differences in how people look at the world.

As before, people are put into their respective Myers-Briggs groups. Thus, all the STs are put in one group, all the NTs in another, and so on. Each group is then told that they are members of the executive committee of a hospital.

The hospital has only one dialysis machine for life support. Unfortunately, six people need to use the machine if they are to live. But since only one person can use it, the other five are in effect consigned to die. Each group is to choose which person gets to use the machine. Most important of all, each group is to describe the process they used to make their final decision. Needless to say, a matter of life and death brings out, as no other exercise generally does, key differences in how different people perceive and structure their world.

The six candidates for the machine are as follows:

- a 13-year-old girl
- a 6-month-old baby boy

- a 35-year-old mother of two children
- an 85-year-old man
- a 23-year-old convicted murderer
- a 9-month-old baby girl

Although there are frequently important differences in which person the groups select, more often than not all of them select the 35-year-old mother of two. It's how they go about selecting her that's revealing.

STs reduce the problem to a set of scales that are used to score each candidate. That is, each candidate gets a single score on each individual scale. The candidate with the highest total score gets the machine. Typical scales are longevity, number of dependents, earning potential, and age. In other words, STs use a completely impersonal, and for them, objective process for selecting who gets to live. Needless to say, it is anything but an objective process for the other types.

NTs completely flip the problem on its head. They work backward starting with the assumption that each person deserves the machine. In effect, each person receives his or her own special formula, or set of scales, so that he or she ends up getting the machine. In other words, NTs take a broad view of the problem. Only after examining the problem from multiple perspectives do they pick a final set of scales, typically something from the first candidate's set of scales, the second, and so on.

NFs do something completely different. They make their decisions only after they have the opportunity to conduct personal interviews with each candidate, their relatives, dependents, neighbors, and anyone else connected closely with the candidate. The ability to conduct personal interviews is a strict requirement before they can make a final decision. In other words, they use highly personal information in selecting who gets to live or die. NF groups may even want to set up scholarships in the memory of those who didn't get the machines. Most of all, they want to set up annual "days of remembrance" for them.

If any of the groups select the murderer, it is the NFs and SFs. NFs question whether the murderer was rightly or wrongly convicted.

They cannot send a person to his death independently of how well the legal system operates. SFs often make their decision for sparing the murderer on the basis of who is most in need of forgiveness. Indeed, SFs generally decide on a feeling basis who needs the machine the most. As a result, STs often look at how SFs make their decision in absolute wonder!

We cannot emphasize enough that this exercise brings out, as clearly and as sharply as any we know, how differently various types look at the world. To put it mildly, it takes a lot of work in interpersonal dynamics, and even psychotherapy, to get different types to understand and appreciate one another.

The Train Crossing Problem

The Train Crossing Problem is another life-and-death exercise. The basic scenario is that in the past few months, a number of children have lost their lives at an important train crossing. The question is what can be done to make the crossing safer.

STs want to put better gates at the crossings, better on-board speed controls, and warning signals. In other words, STs reduce the problem to one of using today's already existing technology.

In contrast, NTs want to build intelligent smart trains and crossings using new technology. They even want to look to models from other industries such as nuclear power plants and what they use to improve safety.

NTs also raise the larger issue of how people are rewarded. That is, what does the system really value? What good does it do to put better speed regulators on trains and gate crossing guards if engineers are rewarded for beating the schedules? If this is the case, then smart engineers will always figure out a way to beat the system, for example, over-ride the speed regulators, and so on.

NFs want to organize parent groups that at important times of the day will safely walk the children across the tracks. They also want better safety education programs for the parents and children.

SFs take a very personal approach to the problem. They lean toward going house to house in their own neighborhoods urging neighbors to help at the crossings. SF likely raise the issue of grieving as a large component of the problem to be solved. As a result, they want to go to the exact sites where children have been killed and place pictures, mementos, and other personal items to honor the memories of the lives that have been lost. In other words, like 9/11, they want to do what is generally found at the sites of any great personal tragedy.

Once again, the different types react as if each is speaking a different language, and they are! For instance, STs don't understand what problem SFs are "solving." But SFs are not solving a problem, per se. They are dealing with their personal grief and that of the families. If grief is a problem to be managed, and it certainly is to us, then they are indeed solving a problem in the only way that is real to them.

The Ideal Organization

The Ideal Organization is another important exercise.

The Ideal Organization of STs is bureaucracy. If bureaucracies had never been invented, STs would perpetually re-create and invent them.

The Ideal Organization of STs is one where everyone has a fixed and permanent job. There is no uncertainty or ambiguity. Everyone knows what is expected of him or her and how he or she will be judged. In other words, the rules of the game are fixed, fair, and well known.

The Ideal Organization of NTs is a matrix organization. Neither the jobs nor the assignments of people to work-teams are fixed or permanent. As the tasks of the organization vary, so do the assignments of people to teams. That is, the skill levels vary as the tasks change.

The Ideal Organization of NFs is essentially no organization at all. It is one big, happy, free-floating community. People just show up and do what needs to be done. They love the constant variety and unpredictability of it all.

Finally, the Ideal Organization of SFs is a small workplace, a small family where everyone knows everyone else on a personal basis. They all know one another's families and celebrate the special occasions in their lives.

Crisis Management

In a very real sense, we've encountered crises at every step in this book. Each of the fables features a personal and/or an environmental crisis of some kind.

Unfortunately, crises have become a prominent feature of today's high-tech, complex world. As a result, the need to manage crises is more vital than ever. We see Crisis Management as one of the key skills of leadership for every type of organization: for-profit and not-for-profit, and public and private.

The modern field of Crisis Management essentially started in response to the poisoning of Tylenol capsules with cyanide in 1982 in a suburb outside of Chicago. Johnson and Johnson (J&J), the parent company of McNeil Pharmaceuticals—the makers of Tylenol—did a nation-wide recall of all Tylenol capsules. Because of its forthright actions, J&J quickly became a model of how to respond to a crisis. Essentially, because of its corporate credo, J&J put consumer safety and health over corporate profits.

Since Ian had worked with the executives of McNeil Pharmaceuticals before the poisonings, he quickly became involved in developing the field of Crisis Management. He has remained involved ever since.

Four major factors are critical to managing crises: (1) types, (2) phases, (3) systems, and (4) stakeholder assumptions.

Types refers to the fact that there are distinctly different types of crises. There are economic (recessions, drop in stock prices, drops in corporate and personal incomes), environmental (oil spills), natural (earthquakes, hurricanes, fires, tornados), hazardous (chemical fires, explosions), informational (computer break-ins), security, ethical breaches, governmental (approval of faulty drugs), media, criminal (sabotage, shootings, product tampering), and public relations.

It has been shown repeatedly that no major crisis is *ever* a single crisis. If not managed properly, any one of the types can set off any other type. That is, any crisis can be the cause or effect of any other. For this reason, one should never plan for single crises in isolation. At a minimum, one must bring Intuiting Thinking and Intuiting Feeling dimensions to bear in planning for crises. One must connect the dots when it comes to thinking and planning for crises.

To do this, one must practice critical thinking at a high level. For instance, by definition, every major crisis starts and/or ends as a public relations disaster.

But one also needs Sensing Thinking dimensions in that one must look at the detailed capabilities as well as the strengths and weaknesses of an organization and take specific steps to better prepare the organization for any and all types of crises. One also needs Sensing Feeling dimensions in that crises take a huge personal toll on the emotional and physical health of an organization, its members, their families, and communities, not to mention all the other stakeholders. When multiple stakeholders are considered, they then comprise a community and that requires the consideration of NF dimensions.

One must also be secure in the sense of attachment theory, which we discuss shortly, to even think about the possibility of crises. To put it mildly, just contemplating crises raises enormous anxiety for many people. One needs to confront denial head-on. In today's world, the unthinkable can happen to any organization anywhere at any time.

The second factor, Phases, refers to the fact that crises unfold over time. Long before most crises occur, they send out a repeated trail of early warning signals. If those signals can be picked, amplified, and acted on, and then many—but not all—crises can be prevented before they occur. But this obviously calls for use of the Extraverted Perceiving dimensions, for one must be oriented to the external world to be aware of and act on these signals.

There are also different kinds of signals that are based on different Myers-Briggs types. If one looks for signals that might come from information on the personal computers of individuals in an organization, one is drawing upon the IST dimensions. If one taps into listening for gossip as an early warning signal, then one is drawing upon the ISF and ESF dimensions. If one uses remote-sensing devices to pick up signals in dangerous situations, then one is drawing upon both EST and ENT dimensions. Monitoring special interest groups brings ESF and ENF into play.

The second factor also includes having appropriate, well-designed damage-control mechanisms in place long before a crisis occurs to prevent the crisis from getting worse. No matter how well prepared an organization is, crises will still occur. As BP showed the world, being reactive only makes crises worse. This means that all the Myers-Briggs types have a crucial role to play in damage control.

Research data show that if an organization is proactive, if it is crisis prepared, then it experiences significantly fewer crises and is more profitable than those organizations that are not well prepared and thereby crisis prone. Crisis-prepared organizations recover faster with fewer injuries or lawsuits. The preparation one puts into crises also improves the day-to-day operations of the business. Crisis Management is not only the right ethical thing to do (SF, NF) but also good for business (ST measures the impacts on immediate, short-term profits; NT measures the impacts on long-term profits and market-share).[6]

The third factor, Systems, includes training Crisis Management Teams (CMT) at corporate and other appropriate divisional levels of an organization. Conflict management is key since all the members of the CMT (CEO, CFO, Chief Legal Officer, COO, Head of Security, HR, Public Affairs, Information Technology) must work together. That is, while they need to challenge one another's assessment of a situation and what to do, they must also work toward a collaborative response.

The most critical part of Systems is the Freudian defense mechanisms. If a culture is full of denial, then it won't prepare for any crises at all. If it uses disavowal, then it will say to itself that the impact of crises is small, and therefore it doesn't need to prepare for them. If it uses grandiosity, then it will say it's culture is so powerful it can withstand anything. If it uses idealization, then it will delude itself into believing that good organizations don't have crises. And, if it uses projection and splitting, it will blame its crises on others. As a result, it won't learn and be better prepared next time,. And surely there will be a next time.

For this reason, even though we don't believe in single variable (SF, ST) explanations for complex phenomena (NT, NF), if we had to pick one, it would be Freudian Defense Mechanisms.

The last factor, Stakeholders, includes incorporating all those stakeholders that can affect and will affect an organization's crises and crisis plans (NT, NF). We leave the reader to figure out how

Life Skills, the Myers-Briggs, Conflict Styles, and Freudian Defense Mechanisms enter in here.

Attachment Theory

Because it's one of the most sensitive topics of all, we've saved Attachment Theory for the very end. Attachment Theory goes deeper than the Myers-Briggs to get at important psychological differences that are not seen as easily. Even though it is a very sensitive topic, it is important nevertheless for anyone who seeks to lead a group. It is important to have at least a basic understanding of the different forms of attachment and how these forms of attachment impact adult relationships.

The theory was essentially invented during World War II in Great Britain when large numbers of children were separated from their parents for long periods of time. During WWII, a great many children were sent out of London to the countryside to help ensure their safety by removing them from the frequent bombings of the city by German planes. Many children were also orphaned. Others were separated from their parents for numerous reasons such as hospital stays.

The effects on the children were generally devastating. When they were first separated, they cried for hours on end, but since good care was not always available or forthcoming, after a while, many just gave up. They showed little if any feeling or emotions. In effect, they shut down completely.

The British psychiatrist, John Bowlby, is generally credited with discovering/inventing Attachment Theory.[7] Bowlby and his colleagues discovered that there were essentially four different styles of caregiving and that these had a tremendous influence on the behavior of people over the entire course of their lives.

Even though Attachment Theory was basically developed to help explain the behavior of very young children, it has since been extended and shown to apply across the entire life span and hence to adults as well.[8]

There are two basic dimensions to the theory: Avoidance and Anxiety. (Attachment Theory's sense of Avoidance is related to that of Conflict Styles in that both are concerned with avoiding highly sensitive interpersonal issues. The big difference is that Attachment Theory's sense of Avoidance goes much deeper.) Given that one can be either high or low on each dimension, there are therefore four resultant Attachment Styles.

If one is low on Avoidance and low on Anxiety, this means that one is relatively secure around other people and furthermore one does not avoid close interpersonal relationships. Accordingly, this style is called Secure. Needless to say, to appreciate all the Myers-Briggs types, one has to be relatively Secure. Similarly, collaboration also demands that one be Secure as well.

The first caretakers of Secure types—when Bowlby wrote, this was generally the mother—are themselves relatively Secure. They are generally not anxious of the prospect of being around others so that they don't pass anxiety onto their children. In addition, they are not generally avoidant in that they don't avoid close interpersonal relationships.

One of the key points about Attachment Theory is that all of this is pre-verbal. That is, the basic models that one learns in relating to others happen unconsciously in the first months and years of life. The mother does not necessarily communicate her fears consciously or verbally. They are passed onto the child by such interactions as how the mother holds and looks at the child, how she reacts when the child cries or misbehaves.

If one is high on Avoidance but low on Anxiety, then on the surface at least, one doesn't need other people. (Deep down, it is another matter.) In effect, one gave up early as a child in getting what one needed from one's caretakers. As a result, one learned not to rely on other people. Accordingly, this style is called Avoidant. Unfortunately, many leaders who appear decisive and confidant share this style. They make tough decisions because they don't really care about the effects of their decisions on others. In many of the fables, King Friday acts an Avoidant. Nonetheless, we get glimpses that he would really like to be Secure but doesn't know how to be so.

If one is high on Anxiety but low on Avoidance, then one is needy. This style is called Anxious. In effect, one has not given up searching for what did not get as a child from one's caretakers, that is, unqualified love and acceptance. Unfortunately, many of those who are needy end up marrying or working for Avoidants who take advantage of them. The unspoken contract is, you the needy take care of relationships—people in general—while I take care of business. Can you see this in many of the fables as well?

Anxious Avoidants are high on both Avoidance and Anxiety and so have the worst of both worlds.

In an important PhD study, "Attachment, Group Functioning and Leadership: An Empirical Study," Christopher G. Bresnahan of the University of Southern California showed that one's leadership style is correlated significantly with one's Attachment style. Thus, Secure types considered more options and people's feelings before making an important decision.[9]

Attachment Theory should be understood by those in leadership positions. However, Attachment Theory is not, like some of the other techniques we have described, a technique to be used for group problem solving. To be as clear as possible, we specifically do not recommend putting all those who are anxious or exhibit high anxiety into a group as a way to examine a problem. Such groupings would not be productive and could be regarded as unethical.

Capstone Exercise

Now that you have read each of the topics and ideally you've participated in each of the previous exercises, please take a problem that you are currently facing in your personal life and/or organization and analyze it from each of the various topics in this chapter. How does the problem/solution appear from the standpoint of each topic? Is it the same?

Figure 16.5 is a list of the Seven Cs and the associated topics, not necessarily in the order in which they were discussed, that we presented in this chapter. The reader is strongly encouraged to explore the linkages between each of the topics and the Seven Cs.

Note that we have abbreviated the Myers-Briggs Personality Styles and Types as
MB Personality Styles in Figure 16.5.

How does each of the topics contribute to the knowledge and use of the Seven Cs?

128 • Putting the Seven Cs to Work

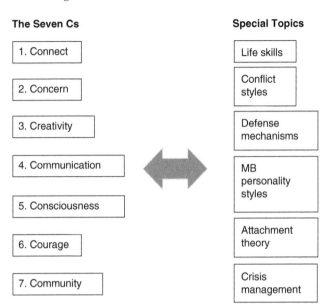

Figure 16.5 Relationships Between the Seven Cs and Special Topics

In order to help you understand the relationships between the Seven Cs and the special topics, we recommend that you perform the following exercises. Your course instructor may or may not require these exercises as class assignments so we urge you to work through them in either case because your understanding and ability to apply the special topics will be greatly enhanced.

1. The situation: There is someone in your life with whom you are having an ongoing problem. The person may be a member of your family or someone with whom you work. Your task is to explain the problematic situation using one or two of the special topics outlined in this chapter. You may choose to write the person a letter or you may choose to write out the conversation you wish to have. As you describe the situation using the analytic tools discussed in this chapter, try to give a balanced presentation that considers the other person's point of view along with your own and avoid being angry or blameful. Conclude the letter or conversation with suggestions for what

YOU have learned from the analysis and what YOU can and will do to make things better.
2. The situation: Select a current important social problem. We suggest texting or talking on cell phone while driving an automobile. These behaviors are known to cause accidents and are receiving considerable attention from law enforcement and policy makers. And yet, the public continues to practice these behaviors and tends to believe that *accidents might happen to others but not to me because I am more careful.* Make use of at least two of the special topic areas to analyze these social problems. Use your analysis to develop suggestions for policy makers that will help them get the public to stop engaging in these dangerous behaviors.

CHAPTER 17

Planet Purple vs. Planet Prism Revisited

Before You Read This Chapter

Before you read this chapter, please go back and re-read "The Story of Planet Purple" in Chapter 8 and our interpretation of it in Chapter 9. Then, think about how you would apply the concepts and ideas in Chapter 16 to analyze the *story further*.

Also, for ease of analysis, we have deliberately repeated many of the essentials details here so that the reader does not have to flip back and forth in order to follow and understand the discussion.

Further Interpretation of *The Story of Planet Purple*

As we noted in Chapter 8, "The Story of Planet Purple" was told in the NMB many years ago to help children appreciate the "delights to be found in human differences"[1] In terms of the concepts and ideas of the last chapter, the story is about the need for all organizations to have the right mix of people who span the range of different Myers-Briggs types and conflict styles.

Only in this way will an organization have the basic psychological skills and attitudes it needs to address complex problems. Indeed, the ability to address all problems from multiple perspectives is the very essence of critical thinking and feeling. And especially in today's world, critical thinking is one of the most important skills and ability any person or organization can have.

In assessing her personality type, recall that Ms. Fairchilde is a highly skilled employee who has demonstrated that she is both a challenger and an adventurer. The adventurer part of her is decidedly N (she is not afraid of new things and ideas; indeed she relishes them). The highly skilled part of her can be both S and N depending on the type of skill that is required for a particular job. It can even be T or F depending upon whether intellectual or emotional skills are required.

The challenger aspect is part of the makeup of a competitive type. The point is that she is, like all of us, a complex person.

Recall also that her current assignment is to explore different models for the design of her organization. (Recall the Ideal Organization exercise.) She is very excited when she comes upon P.P., Inc. She feels that she has found something new. This also is clearly N.

In her feeling that there is a beautiful simplicity about a place where there are no disagreements, no competition, and no differences of opinion about the long-term goals, that is, "the dreams of the organization," Ms. Fairchilde could equally be acting as an ST and/or SF conflict avoider. ST avoiders don't like conflict between ideas and SF avoiders don't like interpersonal conflict. Again, the point is that people are complex and that using the concepts and ideas of the last chapter *in explicit combination with one another* allows us to give a deeper interpretation of people and organizations.

Notice that Ms. Fairchilde's feeling that there is a *beautiful simplicity* about Planet Purple could also be a case of sheer projection.

Ms. Fairchilde may be projecting what she wants to see, not what Planet Purple is actually like. To filter out one's projections from reality requires that we share our perceptions with others who can challenge them without demeaning or destroying us, or our ideas, in the process. At a minimum, this requires that one be aware of one's conflict style so that one doesn't trample over others.

The fact that Ms. Fairchilde wants to share this discovery with her colleagues is a strong indication of the Extrovert dimension. But once again, she may also be projecting that they are open and interested enough to want to learn new things when in reality they are not.

Ms. Fairchilde does not seem to realize that merely by coming to P.P., Inc., asking questions, and exploring their operations, she has already begun to perturb the whole system, that she is disrupting the status quo. This might be an example of outright denial. The fact that she arrives dressed like an emissary from another world in an advanced energy-saving vehicle and she is dressed to the hilt in a white designer suit is certainly an example of not thinking through one's potential impacts. Ideally, F types would be sensitive to this. This behavior indicates that, even though some aspects of her personality lean toward the F type, she is really not a pure F. We might even stretch the point and conclude that she is engaging in denial and/or compartmentalization.

The fact that most members of P.P., Inc.'s staff want nothing to do with her (they run and hide) can be interpreted as a sign that the staff is largely Introverted. In terms of Attachment Theory, the case can also be made that they are extremely Anxious types. The three individuals who are not frightened and are intrigued is a sign of psychological security. This is very important, for it is not enough just to be an N. To be able to act on new and adventuresome ideas, one also has to be Secure. This interpretation is strengthened by the fact that they decide to follow Ms. Fairchilde back to corporate headquarters to learn more about the way things are done there.

As we said in Chapter 9, symbolically, Ms. Fairchilde has come upon an old-fashioned, overly socialized, repressive organization in which employees exist in a state of suspended or arrested development. The repressiveness of these kinds of organizations is symbolized by the lack of color. There is no diversity in them. We are dealing with an almost pure ST organization.

This conclusion is strengthened further by the fact that there is a complete lack of integration between the mind (T) and the body (F) as the use of the "thinking way" of traveling and the rule about rocking demonstrate. As we noted in Chapter 9, feelings and emotions are kept not only completely apart from thoughts and thinking in general but also denigrated altogether. Feelings and emotions are considered inferior to the point that they don't deserve any role in the organization.

Once again, the intrigue that Ms. Fairchilde feels when she first comes upon P.P., Inc. is akin to the desire that many of us have to be in a place where we know exactly what to do and how to do it. This is an indication of the desire to be in a protected Sensing-Thinking environment and to be in a Sensing-Feeling organization as well. The all-too-frequent refrain that "I just want to go to work and do my job; I don't want to have to deal with all that brainstorming and political stuff" is a strong expression of denial and compartmentalization. This is the psychological state of mind that wants to run and hide when anything new comes along. It can also be an expression of Avoidance.

The three individuals who decide to follow Ms. Fairchilde back to her corporate headquarters are different from the others on Planet Purple. They represent the kinds of people (or those parts of every person) who are ready to give up the childish dream that one can live, survive, and thrive in a state of suspended Sensing-Feeling or Sensing-Thinking development. They are ready to grow up, which in Myers-Briggs terms means to integrate all of the Myers-Briggs aspects within one's person. They are ready to integrate mind (T) and body (F) as illustrated by their exploration of their senses. The power of exploring what it is to be a total full, human being (i.e., Myers-Briggs) is expressed when Paul learns to cry (F) and Albert the rabbit says, "Then you've just started to live"—a very NF observation.

When Paul and Pauline decided to return to P.P., Inc., they brought back a model for a different way to organize their workplace and their lives in general (SF and NF). They brought back a model in which each individual could be different (SF and NF).

Recall how Fred put it: "Transitions are almost always signs of growth, but they can bring feelings of loss. To get somewhere new, we may have to leave somewhere else behind."

Changing the culture of P.P., Inc. was not easy: "Some people didn't like some things and other people didn't like other things." Change caused conflict. There will always be some who take longer to embrace change (or a new level of adulthood), and there will always be some who simply resist it and choose to stay in a cocoon-like existence (ST or SF). Again, for some individuals, that is not only their choice but also the right one.

As we noted, in the world we live in today, very few Planet Purple organizations can continue to exist as they have been. The world today is struggling with a fundamental choice between two very different types of organizations. We call these Planet Purple (ST) versus Planet Prism (NF and SF) organizations.

As we also noted, Planet Prism organizations understand that people work primarily to find meaning and purpose (SF, NF) in their lives. Planet Prism organizations understand that by doing well for the environment and adopting socially worthy causes that improve the state of the world (NF), they are thereby doing well for themselves as well (ST). They understand that people want to work for organizations that do good. Planet Prism organizations make their members feel good about themselves.

Notice how the seven essential life skills described in Chapter 16 reinforce these same conclusions. Like all complex human beings, even though she is far from perfect, Ms. Fairchilde blends all of the skills and also does relatively well with them. She is certainly adept at communicating, making connections, perspective-taking, and critical thinking. And she certainly excels in taking on challenges, as do the Pauls and Paulines who followed her.

Changing organizations is one of the most difficult problems people, and organizations themselves, face. Examining the processes of change through the lens of our four special topics helps to explain why that is true.

Concluding Remarks

Let us restate the conclusions of Chapter 9 in terms of the personality types:

1. To attain the illusion of complete control (ST), one must give up one's uniqueness (F); everyone must think, act, and be the same (T).
2. One must be disconnected from one's body (ST) and feelings (SF, NF). One must be compartmentalized; that's why rocking, let alone crying, was not permitted on Planet Purple.
3. And one must believe that everything, for example, space travel, can be accomplished through thinking (T) alone; once again, one must be disconnected from one's feelings. In other words, only thinking matters.

In contrast, Planet Prism organizations are the epitome of integration and connectedness between our brains, our bodies, our feelings, and our souls and spirits.

CHAPTER 18

Good Friends Revisited

The story of "Good Friends" is fundamentally about perspective-taking and communication. When Lady Aberlin realizes that she forgot her promise to take Daniel with her to the picnic, she readily apologizes. Her apologies don't help to make Daniel feel better. In fact, he gets somewhat defensive after she says, "I'm really sorry, Daniel." He asks "Are you? Are you really?" It isn't until Lady Aberlin stops to see the situation from his perspective by asking, "Does it make you feel like we're not really friends when you hear that I just forgot to come and pick you up?" that Daniel feels understood. After this moment of perspective-taking, he is ready to accept her explanation and apology.

Daniel is so emotionally engaged in the situation that he cannot communicate his point of view to Lady Aberlin. She needs to "listen" to more than his words; she needs to hear his nonverbal communication.

These two points are summed up at the end when Daniel sings about an important way to say "I love you," that is, to take time to really understand how another person feels.

Think about how the different Myers-Briggs types would respond to how Daniel felt when Lady Aberlin forgot to pick him up in a timely manner. Like the Train Crossing Exercise, STs typically respond by getting Daniel and Lady Aberlin better real-time communication pagers or devices. NTs suggest that they both need to wear "new communication helmets or even 'intelligent blouses or shirts' with communication devices built into them." While both are meant to be helpful, in psychological terms, they miss the real heart of the story.

As we said in Chapter 10, we believe that the heart of the fable's message is to learn to listen for the feelings (F) behind the words (S). This is deep communication—and perspective-taking. The particular words a colleague uses when he or she is stressed may not actually describe the pain he or she is really feeling. Daniel kept asking Lady Aberlin to explain *why* (ST, NT) she had forgotten him, but what he really wanted to know was *how* could he trust their friendship (F) if he could so easily be forgotten. Only when Lady Aberlin stops offering logical explanations (ST, NT), hears Daniel's deep feeling (NF *and* SF), and articulates it for him, he can relax and let go of his anger. In other words, Daniel can let go of his deep anxiety. Indeed, Daniel is a prime, archetypal example of an anxious type.

Recall that the second important message of the story is about learning to accurately name our feelings. Accurately naming feelings is not a matter of ST but of SF and NF. When we accurately name a feeling, we can react more appropriately in terms of Myers-Briggs and conflict styles.

When Lady Aberlin told Daniel about the time a friend forgot to come to her birthday party, Daniel asked if she felt mad about her friend forgetting. Lady Aberlin clarifies in SF and NF terms for Daniel that what she felt was not anger but disappointment (F). This clarification (SF, NF) is very important because how one reacts to disappointment is very different from how one reacts to anger. Learning to name feelings (SF, NF), to recognize the subtle distinctions between, for example, anxiety and fear or guilt and shame, is an important aspect of emotional intelligence (SF, NF). If we haven't learned to make distinctions between basic feelings, we are likely to react inappropriately and escalate emotional situations. We are likely to turn it into an inappropriate conflict situation by using an inappropriate conflict and/or Myers-Briggs style.

The third important message in the story is about *identifying the triggering feeling*. Identifying triggering feelings can help us appropriately label (SF, NF) the emotion being felt. When something happens that causes us to feel angry; for example, Daniel's presenting emotion to Lady Aberlin was anger, however when, with Lady Aberlin's help (F), he stopped to retrace the situation to locate the triggering event, he discovered that what he felt was abandonment.

A technique for identifying triggering feelings is to engage in the process that we called "Rewind Your Mind." This entails stepping back long enough to play the situation backward (N) to the point at which emotions (F) begin to take over. When that moment is discovered, we can often label the feeling and react more appropriately. Learning to rewind your mind and help your colleagues do the same can help to take some of the heat (i.e., destructive conflict) out of the workplace.

Notice carefully that retracing and rewinding are examples of NF. They are N because we are reexamining something in a different context. They are also F because we don't do it in a completely detached, or analytical, way (T). This is not to say that NT does not and cannot play an important role in getting us to think differently. It does. But the important thing to understand is that NT plays a supporting role. It is not the main player.

However, from the standpoint of critical thinking, the situation is different. Here, NT plays a major role. This is why it is so important to analyze crucial situations from more than one framework or perspective because they often reveal different facets and conclusions. It is rarely, if ever the case, that one and only one interpretation or analysis is right or the whole of a situation.

The story also illustrates that talking about difficult feelings can be therapeutic. In other words, children need to connect (E) with others (NF) so that they can express their deepest fears, joys, hopes, and dreams.

Adults Have the Same Needs

Once again, as we noted throughout, adults have the same needs. Planet Prism organizations have learned how to address this need in innovative (N) ways. For instance, employees regularly get together to read and to share different books on human development, individual and organizational health, and important social issues. That is, they don't just read books about business. They read and talk about people.

Planet Prism organizations regularly invite (E) nationally recognized experts in management (ST, NT, NF) to spend at least an entire day interacting (communicating) with employees, customers, and other major stakeholders, to gain an outside perspective

(perspective taking) and a critique (critical thinking) of the organization. Prior to their arrival, employees are encouraged to read and to discuss their works and their ideas in small groups (Myers-Briggs). By inviting outsiders with different and conflicting points of view, the organizations are continually open to new ideas. They are also teaching how to use conflict constructively.

An Example

Recall the example from Donna's work experience when she worked as the head of broadcast standards for a major TV network. She had the responsibility for insuring that the content of children's TV programs not only was appropriate (SF, NF) but also actually aided their health and development (SF, NF). The programs certainly were not supposed to cause harm.

Donna struggled constantly with getting the producers and writers of children's TV programs to go along with her mandate. However, they just wanted to produce and to write exciting shows that would "bring in the numbers," in this case the audience. Where Donna was thinking in terms of SF and NF (the emotional development of the children who watched the shows, i.e., the seven essential life skills), the producers and writers were concerned almost exclusively with ST (i.e., increasing the numbers of viewers, and thereby the money the shows would make).

When the horrific Columbine shootings occurred—precisely because they were so tragic—they provided a "teachable moment" to reach the producers and writers (SF, NF). They provided an opportunity to "connect" with the writers and producers about the importance of making shows that helped young children to grow and to develop in healthy ways. That is, they were able to shift from an exclusively ST to an SF, NF mode. They could relate to the broader social consequences of their shows.

Recall also that after the Columbine shootings, Donna also invited leading experts on the development of boys to conduct a one-day training seminar. The organization was open (N) to inviting in outsiders (E).

We cannot emphasize enough that the principle of connectedness (ENF), or reaching out, needs to be continually encouraged and broadened. The list of "mentors," "coaches," and "outside influences" that workers and managers are exposed to should be expanded to include experts on male and female psychology and emotional development so that everyone can continue to grow. In this way our organizations can truly become learning and growing neighborhoods.

Concluding Remarks

Planet Prism organizations incorporate connectedness in deep and meaningful ways. It is deeply embedded in and is a fundamental part of their everyday operations. They use connectedness as their primary criterion in selecting prospective members. Recall that on a cross-country flight on Southwest Airlines (SWA), Ian struck up a conversation with one of the flight attendants. She confirmed that SWA does indeed "select for attitude (F); train for skills (T)."

Recall as well that SWA's selection process begins by inviting prospective members to attend a meeting with thirty or so other people. Prospective members are asked open-ended questions, such as "Tell me about a time when you went beyond what was expected of you as part of your normal job." While the interviewers are certainly interested in the verbal responses to the questions, they are even more interested in nonverbal responses. They are looking for the demonstrated ability of prospective members to "connect instantly" in a group of complete strangers. To put it mildly, this is a prime example of ESF and ENF.

Once again, SWA is not a typical airline or business, but that's not the main point of the story. The main point is that SWA represents the future of all companies and is the model for Planet Prism organizations.

No matter what their main products or services are, all companies are now in the service or F business. Zappos Shoes is just one example of a business that understands this. Everyone needs to connect with customers and to each other both inside (I) and outside (E) of the organization. Every organization needs to learn how to become more SF and NF. At the same time, they also need to retain and to upgrade their ST and NT skills. Again, it is not an either/or but a both/and situation.

CHAPTER 19

No Bare Hands in This Land Revisited

As we've discussed, rules are important. Sensible, reasonable rules provide boundaries and a form of security and predictability that actually enables greater freedom. However, unreasonable, unpredictable rules create a completely different environment. In the case of King Friday's rule about mittens, we see a perfect example of how rules that seem arbitrary can thwart constructive use of the Essential Skills. King Friday may have designed the new rule for the day out of concern (F) for his subjects/employees, but his way of imposing (introverted T, competitive) the new rule shows his inability to use perspective-taking. He demonstrates no effort to figure out what the others think and feel or how his imposition of a seemingly arbitrary rule will impact their work. His action also inadvertently inhibits critical thinking by everyone except Lady Elaine. Instead of questioning a rule that prevented them from completing their current tasks (work assignments), they simply stop and put on their mittens. By being competitive, Lady Elaine stands up to King Friday's autocratic behavior and demands to know "why you have made this rule." She persists even after she feels the impact of the hand-freezing breeze. Had King Friday considered the perspective of his subjects, he might not have turned this into a hot issue that led to loss of valuable work time and to a degree of defensiveness from one of his important subjects. What type of employee would you rather have, one who simply accepts a dictum that leads to work stoppage or one who challenges something that comes with no reasonable explanation?

In terms of the Myers-Briggs, in today's world of highly educated workers, the CEO—the King!—can't behave as ISTJ and expect to get away with it. Without taking others into account (E), he can't just issue his own (I) narrow set of rules and edicts (ST) at will (J) and expect them to be followed blindly. He has to take the feelings (F) of others (E) into account and explain the purpose (NT, NF) for the rules. As we said, rules that don't make sense are senseless. Remember, good organizations make good rules not only *for* their members but also *with* (E) their members (SF, NF).

Myers-Briggs Rules

Let's look at how the different Myers-Briggs types conceive of rules.

For STs, rules are like strict laws that permit no exceptions. Everyone must obey them strictly or suffer the penalties. The ideal of STs is to have specific rules for everything that is important. At their best, their rules lay out what's acceptable and what's not acceptable in an organization so that there are no misunderstandings. STs excel at figuring out the derailed complexities of an organization.

STs are completely right when they insist that without any rules, chaos would ensue. They are also right when they point out that it is misguided and naïve to think that organizations and society could run without rules. Without rules, we would descend into a state of anarchy. But they are wrong when they think that one can make rules that can cover every conceivable situation.

ISTs make rules out of their own experience (I) without considering anyone else. Ps have difficulty on settling on any set of rules. And Js quickly settle on a single set of rules.

For NTs, rules are merely suggestive guidelines that must be carefully designed to help people and systems achieve important goals. In other words, rules are tools, not inviolable laws. As such, rules must be constantly reviewed, and revised if need be, to keep up with the changing times.

For an SF/NF like Fred, rules and discipline are a loving gift that parents give to their children when their children need them. Fred understood that children desperately need and want clear-cut limits and rules. That is, they need clear ST boundaries. They need and want appropriate discipline as well. But the ST rules have to be tempered and administered with SF, NF feeling and love.

Conflict Style Rules

Competitive types view rules as a contest, a game, to see who can take control of a situation. Fairness has nothing to do with it, only winning.

Accommodators and avoiders view rules as losing proposition. It is a contest in which they are perpetual losers.

Compromisers and collaborators, on the other hand, see rules as an opportunity for people to take control of their lives such that everyone wins.

A Common Misperception

As we said in Chapter 11, because Fred was thoroughly genuine and loving, caring, and accepting—a very strong F—there is a common misperception that he was, therefore, permissive toward children's behavior, that he advocated no rules, discipline, or limits when it came to raising children. Nothing could be further from the truth.

Fred knew that we showed our love for our children through demonstrating what was expected of them and what the consequences (ST) were if they didn't meet those expectations. To think that healthy children and adults would result without sensible rules and appropriate discipline goes against every grain of research on children.

As we also noted, Planet Prism organizations have clear-cut rules (ST) regarding employee misconduct, aggressiveness, and violence in the workplace.[1] From Day One, Planet Prism organizations make it perfectly clear that sexually offensive jokes or those featuring violence will not be tolerated for one instant. They have a zero tolerance policy with regard to sexual harassment and workplace violence. Anyone violating these rules is sent immediately to counseling to determine whether they are still fit to remain in the organization.

Because rudeness and incivility have become such important problems, let's look at how Plant Prism organizations respond to them through the lenses of the Myers-Briggs and the like:

- Plant Prism organizations have zero tolerance policies; they make it perfectly clear that rudeness and incivility will not be tolerated under any circumstances. One instance is one too many. To put it mildly, this is a clear-cut example of the appropriate and constructive use of STJ.
- They take an honest look in the mirror. They ask themselves, "What is it about our culture (NF) that has encouraged or turned a blind eye toward incivility; do we promote in subtle and not-so-subtle ways those who are rude; in other words, are we to blame?" Taking a look at oneself—at the larger system and culture—is an example of NT, NF. It is a case of being secure enough to be honest with oneself. It is also a clear-cut example of perspective taking.
- They weed out trouble before it enters their organization. They ask prospective members for their permission to talk with previous employers; they probe for underlying reasons why the person left their previous position. They ask the prospective member whether they will allow them to ask their previous employer questions with regard to rudeness and incivility. This is as good an example one could ever hope to find of using *all* of the Myers-Briggs types.
- They teach civility. It is not enough to be against rudeness and incivility; to root it out, one has to be for something positive. This is clearly SF and NF.
- They put their ear to the ground and listen carefully for any signs that incivility and rudeness are taking root in their organization (ST, NT, NF, and SF).
- When incivility occurs, they react immediately and forcefully; they don't wait for days to pass before they respond to uncivil acts; the goal is a "just in time" policy with regard to positive and negative behaviors. This is clearly J.
- They heed early warning signals. Acts of incivility send out early warning signals long before they occur, in the form of increased absenteeism, workplace sabotage, etc. The best organizations

are constantly on the lookout for early warning signs of rudeness and incivility (ST, NT, NF, and SF). In other words, they are practicing good, proactive crisis management before a crisis happens.
- They don't make excuses for powerful instigators of incivility; the higher a person is in the organization, the less tolerance he or she has with regard to incivility. This is important because research has shown that incivility tends to travel downward. In unhealthy organizations, those on top are uncivil toward insubordinates, but not vice versa. They don't allow the king and his princes and princesses any special latitude. This is NT, NF. Depending on how it is done, it can be ST and SF as well.
- They invest heavily in post-departure interviews. It is estimated that annually anywhere between 20 and 25 percent of people leave organizations each year because of rudeness and incivility. Rudeness and incivility seriously hamper the bottom line. Exit interviews are thus a valuable way of taking a final look in the mirror (SF, NF).

While the Myers-Briggs may not explain everything—no single instrument or theory can—it explains a lot about organizations.

CHAPTER 20

The Bass Violin Festival Revisited

"The Bass Violin Festival" provides beautiful examples of the Essential Life Skills. Consider making connections. When the subjects of the NMB came to the conclusion that they could make what they do well work as contributions to the festival, they showed their ability to make creative, interesting, unique, and useful connections out of the assignment. They worked from and with the right side of the brain.

Taking on challenges

New challenges can be stressful. We see the subjects of the NMB are expressing stress when they meet to share their frustrations.

Whether or not King Friday intended this to be a stretch assignment is open to debate, but the truth is that the subjects were on the verge of unproductive stress.

Self-directed, engaged learning

When the subjects of the NMB discovered ways to bring their social, emotional, and cognitive skills together as they reinterpreted the assignment, they became self-directed, engaged learners. Their enthusiasm was palpable. They enacted the value that comes from being part of a community of learners. Did the king/CEO knowingly facilitate the progression of his subjects/employees from frustrated to self-directed, engaged learners? Does King Friday himself represent a self-directed, engaged learner? Does he model good leadership? Why/why not?

To go back even further, recall that the story starts with the CEO, King Friday, announcing to the staff, that is, his subjects, that he has received a proposal from a complimentary organization, represented by the Mayor of Southwood, for a partnership. It is clear that as the CEO, King Friday wants the partnership to proceed without taking his subjects into account. As such he is acting as an ISTJ.

The king also wants NMB, Inc. to be the lead company. In other words, as a highly competitive type, he wants the whole pie so-to-speak. To accommodate the king's wishes, all of the subjects must develop a plan (NT) to make the king's expertise (ST) the central element of the partnership. The subjects are dubious and anxious, because they realize that the CEO is the sole expert in NMB's "technology" (T), and they also realize intuitively that NMB's technology is not, in and of itself, sufficient for the proposed partnership. That is, T may be necessary, but it is not sufficient without the appropriate buy-in (F) and accompanying skills (T) of the staff to accomplish the task. Their frustration, that is, anxiety, is exacerbated when the CEO presents one senior staff member with a newer version of the technology (NT) and thinks that this "fine instrument" is what is needed to jump start the process.

Recall that with this act, King Friday commits a mistake that is common in the thinking of far too many organizations. It is the belief (ST) that newer and better technology is always the solution to every problem. In fact, research has shown again and again the complete opposite. Technology alone without the skills, knowledge, and confidence (SF) to use it will not succeed. In fact, technology by itself often increases our fears and makes us painfully aware of our shortcomings, that is, increases our anxiety. Instead of putting us more at ease and making us more proficient, it increases our fears and anxieties—as it did with Lady Aberlin.

Furthermore, adopting a single solution (ST) to a complex problem (NT, NF) as King Friday did leads to the fundamental error of *solving the wrong problem precisely,* that is, the error of the third kind (E3).

This is precisely why the Myers-Briggs is so important. Without looking at any important problem from at least the four Myers-Briggs perspectives, one is virtually guaranteed to commit an E3.

To avoid E3s, or at the least minimize their chances of occurring, people in organizations need to take the time to "play" (NT, NF) with the definition of what the problem(s) really are (NT, NF), or like the characters in the story, the redefinition of the word "play" (NT, NF).

As we also noted, a CEO that is fortunate to have a staff like the characters in the NMB has much to be thankful for. Lady Elaine Fairchilde, Lady Aberlin, Miss Pullificate, and the others redefined the problem and came up with a wide range of creative approaches (NT, NF) to the concept of a bass violin festival. And just as important, the fact that they each found a solution drawn from their individual talents and expertise led to greater involvement and investment in the outcome than a single, imposed solution.

Let us recount the lessons of "The Bass Violin Festival" in terms of the Myers-Briggs:

1. Technology (T) alone is never a substitute for skill (S). The best bass violin in the world, that is, technology, will not make up for the fact that we don't know how to use the technology.
2. By itself, technology often increases our fears (anxiety). It makes us painfully aware of our shortcomings. Instead of putting us more at ease, it increases our fears and anxieties. It makes us feel very uneasy (SF, NF).
3. Often when we are afraid—indeed the more that we are afraid—we project our fears onto others. Instead of owning up to our fears as our own, we blame others. It is easy, and even justified, to blame the predicament entirely on King Friday. After all, he was the one that gave his subjects a seemingly impossible task. But once again, King Friday is not fundamentally responsible for the fears that the subjects feel with regard to their creative ideas. For all that we know, the king intentionally wanted to give his subjects a task that he knew they couldn't complete to see if it would stimulate their creativity and help them to overcome their fears.
4. Creativity also forces us to confront our deepest fears: Are we good enough? Are we liked for who we are (F)? Will we look foolish and be laughed at if we expose our ideas and feelings to the world? Will I be punished and ridiculed for my ideas? The fears really lie within us and not the outside world.

5. Recall that in many myths and fairytales, it is most often the youngest child, the one who is handicapped in some way, who demonstrates the courage to tell the truth (ISF). Where older children and adults have learned to be wary of and accommodate to the world, the youngest child has not learned to distrust his or her inner voice and creativity(INF). The child's innocence is a protective barrier against the harshness of the world.
6. To be creative, we have to be a child again. We have to be childlike (SF) without being childish (NT, NF).

Creativity: To See the World Again as a Child

Recall that a few years ago, a company sent its entire team of top executives to an outside course in creativity. A prominent feature of the course was a module that consisted of going to an art museum and looking at the paintings under the guidance of a docent. Looking at something differently, and especially so-called familiar things, is a prime example of NT and NF.

Recall also that prior to their actual participation in the course, this particular module elicited the most negative response of all the parts of the program (anxiety). After all, what does going to an art museum have to do with business? (This is a typical ISTJ response to something new.) After they took it, all of the executives agreed that it was the most valuable part of the entire program. Why? Because it allowed them to look at familiar things with fresh eyes (NT, NF again). The docent taught the executives how to look at modern art through the eyes of the artists. This allowed them to better understand what the artists were trying to do.

Parent, Adult, Child

To see the world again as a child (SF) is the fundamental basis of creativity. It involves feelings of joy, fun, and play (SF, NF).

Seeing the world again as a child brings us to another important typology, Ego States, which we have not discussed up to this point. Ego States refers to the fact that there are three voices within everyone: Parent, Adult, and Child. In brief, this is a popular version of Freud's Super-ego, Ego, and Id.

The Child is the untamed source of instinctual life-energy with which we are all born. It is the part of us that is forever young. Like a child, it is impulsive and wants to get what it wants immediately.

The Parent is the part of us that says, "No, you can't do that because it's wrong and not good for you." It's the part that sets rules and therefore makes civilized society possible. Which is why there are Parent style rules in addition to Myers-Briggs, Conflict Style rules, and the like.

The Adult is the part that mediates between the Child and the Parent. It says, "Listen to the Parent and then you can have all your goodies." The Adult has to acknowledge and manage both the desires and the demands of the Child and Parent.

Notice that whatever one's Myers-Briggs type, one can be predominantly in one state or another. If one is an ISFP and in the Parent state, then one's attitude is "I'm right and you're wrong." If one is in the Child state, then one's attitude is "You're bigger and more powerful than me so I'll play along with your believing that you're right!"

If one is in the Adult state, then no matter what one's Myers-Briggs type, the attitude is that I need other Myers-Briggs types to complement my one-sidedness. The other types are not a threat.

Notice that the Adult state is necessary for Collaboration.

See if you can figure out how the other two ego states relate to the other conflict styles.

CHAPTER 21

The Reluctant Ring-Bearer Revisited

From the standpoint of Life Skills, Daniel Striped Tiger was unable to communicate his concerns about his role in the upcoming wedding. As the story unfolded, it became clear that his misunderstanding of the role caused him great anxiety. His anxiety is transformed into fear that he will be unable to perform the task and that he will let people down. But that isn't what's really bothering him.

The other side of the communication process is how well Betty Templeton and Lady Aberlin listened. They focused on solving the mechanics of the problem, that is, taping the ring to the pillow. If they had listened more carefully when Daniel said that every time he thinks about being the ring-bearer, the worse it makes him *feel*, they might have helped him sooner. Think of Daniel as an employee who exhibits anxiety after being given an unfamiliar task to perform. Consider how careful listening might help you to help an employee get to the real source of the anxiety

Recall also that Fred was fond of saying that if we wanted to know why a certain person was mean, angry, or sad, then we had to know their story, that is, what made them what they are and what was going in their lives at the present. People don't act randomly. There are always reasons for their behavior, especially all the more that we don't like it. This is the moral of "The Reluctant Ring-Bearer."

Every person is a lifetime of stories. This is clearly SF and NF. To know a person *is* to know his or her stories, for in the beginning and in the end, a person *is* the sum (better yet, the product) of his or her stories. The same is true of organizations.

Conflict is the basis of all stories big and small, positive as well as negative. Organizations are fertile ground for conflict because they are made up of and have to deal with a multitude of stakeholders, that is, all those parties, organizations, and institutions that affect and are affected by an organization and its behavior and policies. The internal stakeholders of an organization are its employees, managers, executives, and board of directors. External stakeholders range from the competition, banks and financial institutions, unions, and state and local governments to the media and national and international governments.

Stakeholders are frequently analyzed, if they are at all, in terms of their power, resources, information, and competitive advantage, that is, from the standpoint of ST and NT. But they are almost never analyzed in terms of SF and NF, Conflict Styles, and Defense Mechanisms. As we shall see in the next chapter, this is critical when it comes to dealing with crises.

At this point, see if you can analyze your organization's (family's) stakeholders in terms of the Myers-Briggs and Conflict Styles. What does your organization (family, society) look like?

CHAPTER 22

Once Upon Each Lovely Day Revisited

Throughout the story King Friday shows that he has trouble with being able to focus and exercise self-control. Instead of paying attention to the problem presented by Handyman Negri, he indulges in his desire to play music and in so doing distracts Negri from his own work. Instead of solving the copier problem, he simply throws the extra copies in the trash, thereby contributing to the problem. Instead of focusing on the mounting garbage problem, he orders nose muffs—a temporary, uncomfortable solution that further distracts people from their work. And then when his subjects arrive at a process for gathering new ideas to deal with the problem, King Friday again fails to focus, choosing to practice his bass violin.

King Friday would not do well on the Marshmallow Test. In contrast, the residents of the NMB do practice focus and self-control. That focus enables them to take on the challenge and make connections between the options available and come up with a solution.

Recall as well from Chapter 13 that the moral of the story is that we need to practice care for the external environment and must never take the environment for granted. Recall further that there is an even deeper moral to the story: if we want to respect and to care for the external environment—Nature—then we have to respect and care for our internal environment, that is, our internal nature, our attitudes toward ourselves (SF, NF) and the world (NT, NF).

Integrating our respect and care for both the external environment and our internal environment is an expression of spirituality. The story teaches other lessons.

For one, King Friday is certainly not connected to his subjects. Indeed, he is profoundly disconnected from them. In terms of the Myers-Briggs, this means that he is once again acting as an ISTJ. E and F are conspicuously absent and/or undeveloped in King Friday. Even though down deep he is lonely, this is still true. Indeed, if his E and F were more developed, then he might not be so lonely. Unfortunately, King Friday is trapped in a vicious circle.

His kingdom is on the verge of drowning in garbage, and all he wants to do is to play music. To say that he avoids the problem is a gross understatement. He uses music both to drown out the problem and as a major diversion. The king is anything but a spiritual leader, in contact with neither his own inner nature nor with that of his subjects. He is, at the very least, in denial of the crisis at hand.

The king doesn't listen, because he doesn't want to hear (ISTJ). In terms of the Myers-Briggs, hearing is ESFP, ENFP. Handyman Negri, a poor subject, a lowly employee (i.e., stakeholder), is begging the king to take action (ESFJ, ENFJ), to listen to and focus on a serious problem, that is, to move beyond denial and to collaborate (ENF) with all the stakeholders in the kingdom. Instead, the king passes the job off to one of his subjects, Lady Aberlin, one of his favorites, a favored stakeholder. The king neglects the safety and health needs of people, which span all the Myers-Briggs types. Because he is not integrated, in terms of Maslow's needs hierarchy, the king can't even attend to the basic, safety, and health needs of his people.

Once again, to say that the king is immature is a gross understatement. At best, he is reactive. He is certainly not proactive. But this means that he is not a "green CEO!"

Until the king stops focusing entirely on himself (IJ), the kingdom is truly rotten and smelly. The nose muffs are a feeble attempt to cover up the surface of the problem by not dealing fully with it; that is, this is denial once again. The fans represent other feeble attempts to avoid dealing fully with the problem.

But the biggest and the most fundamental lesson of the story is that to deal with life's problems, we have to get beyond ourselves (I). We have to discover a bigger purpose in life (NF). That's why the solution is discovered only when the people reach out and help one another (ESF, ENF).

Problems are not and cannot be isolated any more. They affect everyone.

All of the stories that we have considered teach us that the solutions to our problems rarely, if ever, lie solely in bigger and better technology (T). The solutions lie fundamentally deep within us (SF, NF). And the deepest sense of "within us" is spiritual.

All of us are searching for meaning and purpose. All of us want to know why we are here.

As we've previously stated, for Fred Rogers, the word "consciousness" was merely a stepping-stone to the deeper concept of spirituality. And if spirituality means anything, it is not only recognizing and treating the whole person—the whole environment—but also helping us in our search for meaning and purpose.[1]

At our core, all of us are spiritual beings. And the essence of spirituality is wholeness (i.e., *integrated* ST, NT, NF, SF). When we are whole, we are connected to every part of ourselves and to the entire universe. In other words, spirituality is found when we develop and integrate all of Myers-Briggs within others and ourselves.

Recall that surveys constantly reveal that people want to bring their whole person, or the complete package (S & N, T & F, I & E, P & J), to work. They are frustrated with having to leave significant parts of themselves at home when they come to work. The search for wholeness is a critical component in the constant quest for meaning and purpose in one's life.

When people are asked how much of themselves they can bring to work, they report that they can mainly bring only their brains (T), but not their deepest feelings and emotions (F), let alone their souls. Many organizations foster the illusion that one can split reason from feelings and emotions. This illusion is one of the major indignities that people suffer at the hands of organizations. They are forced to split the cognitive or thinking parts of themselves apart from the emotional, ethical, and spiritual.[2]

This has the dire consequence that organizations do not reap the full creativity (NT, NF) of their employees, and employees do not get the opportunity to develop themselves as whole human beings. Their work does not contribute to a sense of who and what they are. In turn, this means that employees cannot relate fully to one another, and hence, even less to their customers.

CHAPTER 23

Daniel Tiger and the Snowstorm Revisited

"Drowning in cereal" is a metaphor for living and working in a world that is filled with distractions and information overload, a world in which the ability to set goals and stick to them is more important than ever. When it is known that the only way to stop the cereal was to get Daniel to return to the clock even though he was terrified to do so, the committee (Lady Aberlin and Neighbor Aber) took on the challenge by engaging in critical thinking to come up with a solution that dealt with both the technical issue (floating through the distracting cereal) and the emotional issue (Daniel's fear). Recall that one of the techniques that spur critical thinking is the acknowledgment of our need for the knowledge that resides in the minds of others. The three friends who work together to solve the problem have created a brain trust that provided reliable, trustworthy information and support.

In terms of the Myers-Briggs, the story of Daniel Tiger is about the importance of being connected with other people (SF, NF). Through our connections with others, we are able to do and be things that we cannot by ourselves. This is another way of saying that we need a brain trust to solve problems. While we know this to be true for young children, it is equally true of the child that is still in each of us.

The fact that the snow in the story is cereal suggests that the tasks that are overwhelming us may be mundane, as mundane as cereal, but they are more than we can handle.

Many of us react just as Daniel did in such a situation—we retreat to a safe place (ISF or with others ESF) and hope (denial) that the problems will just go away on their own. Some of us react the way that King Friday did, that is, by seeking fancy tools to apply to the task (cereal-proof armor and blankets) and/or commanding the job to be done. (This is an ISTJ way of handling the problem.) Both Daniel's approach (avoiding, i.e., running away from the problem) and King Friday's approach (bringing in fancy tools, i.e., technology, and invoking authority) represent extreme ways of dealing with the situation. Neither of these approaches worked because by themselves they were incomplete and one-sided.

Let us reiterate an important point that we made earlier. There is nothing inherently bad or wrong about ST per se. Rather, in their purest forms, each of the types can be wrong or incomplete, especially when they are not integrated with their opposite types.

Notice that only those colleagues who observed what was happening and were capable of working together (ENF) were able to formulate a creative and practical solution (ST) that actually solved the problem.

We cannot emphasize enough that the first step was to pay complete attention to their colleague and to understand what the real underlying fear (anxiety) was that kept him from solving the problem (Daniel was afraid he would drown) and then employ a low-tech, creative tool that dealt with the specific issue at hand (the inflatable boat). The second step was to offer help and support (ESF, ENF) to the colleague until he or she regained control of the situation (the snowing stopped).

The story of Daniel and the Snowstorm is a metaphor for connectedness. When we are connected with others, we are connected with the deepest parts of ourselves. Or, in the words of Fred, "We speak with more than our mouths. We listen with more than our ears."

Connectedness is speaking and listening with our whole being, our whole person (E & I, S & N, T & F). It is speaking and listening—mostly listening—so that we can truly hear another person. It is putting our needs aside so that we can attend to the needs of others. It is listening without judging. It is listening with our heads, our hearts, and most of all, our souls. It is hearing the spirit of another.

CHAPTER 24

Leadership Revisited

In Chapter 15 we stated that the overarching principle of this book is that there is a desperate need to create healthier organizations: organizations that promote the emotional health (SF, NF) of their members. We have a right to expect Planet Prism organizations. We deserve them.

Old-line, hierarchical organizations (ST) are antithetical to the notion of organizations as neighborhoods, that is, where everyone is a member, and not just nameless and faceless employees. The entire philosophy of this book is that it does not have to be this way, that it is possible for us to change to a new model of leadership that will allow, even encourage, greater emotional health among all workers.

Recall the principles of leadership that flow from Fred's ideas.

Principle #1: Everyone is a leader no matter where he or she is in an organization.

If you could only sense how important you are to the lives of those you meet, how important you can be to the people you may never even dream of. There is something of yourself that you leave at every meeting with another person.

—Fred Rogers

This statement does not say that being a leader depends upon one's ST role and status in an ST organization. Rather, it is open to everyone. This is clearly both a Sensing-Feeling and Intuiting-Feeling statement.

> Principle #2: Lifelong self-discovery is a basic requirement of leadership.
>
> Discovering the truth about ourselves is the work of a lifetime, but it's worth the effort.
>
> —Fred Rogers

This is clearly a Sensing-Feeling, Intuiting-Feeling statement that one could ever hope to find.

> Principle #3 Love life and love what you do.
>
> The thing I remember best about successful people I've met through the years is their obvious delight in what they're doing . . . and it seems to have very little to do with worldly success. They just love what they're doing, and they love it in front of others.
>
> —Fred Rogers

It is equally important that a leader help others (ESF, ENF) find the internal switch that will give them the opportunity to experience pleasure and self-fulfillment in their work.

Fred said, "How children feel about themselves *is* what I care about most."

Leadership has to do with how we treat people (SF, NF)—the people we are leading, the people we are following, the shift we have in our roles as leaders or followers, and the importance of sticking to our guiding principles.

> Principle #4: Communication is at the heart of leadership.

Recall the fable of Daniel the Tiger as Ring-Bearer:

Daniel was asked to be the ring-bearer at a wedding in Make-Believe. He was terrified (anxious) at the thought of it. Some of his friends thought it may be because he was worried he couldn't do the job well, that maybe the ring would fall off the pillow, so they taped it on. But even that didn't help. His friends encouraged him to ask questions about the role of a ring-bearer, and he asked if he'd have to wear a "bear" suit (isn't that what a "ring bear" would wear?)—as a timid tiger, he was afraid of bears—even of dressing up as one.

> Listening and trying to understand the needs of those we would communicate with seems to me to be the essential pre-requisite of any real communication. And we might as well aim for *real* communication.
> —Fred Rogers

Real communication is the true goal of leadership. In real communication, the leader conveys acceptance and respect for what a colleague is expressing. Real communication requires the practice of active listening—the opposite of passive listening. When one listens actively, one puts aside his or her own thoughts (IT) and viewpoints (S & N) and strives for empathy (F) with what the speaker is expressing and feeling. Active listening is a skill that can be learned and one that must be practiced. It is a skill that a true leader must have.

> We speak with more than our mouths. We listen with more than our ears.
> —Fred Rogers

Principle #5: To gain power, give it away.

Put real value into play as part of work:

> One of the greatest paradoxes about omnipotence is that we need to feel it early in life, and lose it early in life, to achieve a healthy, realistic, yet exciting, sense of potency later on.
> —Fred Rogers

Contrary to many of our common notions, leadership does not mean omnipotence. It means practicing the essential life skills everyday and helping others as well. And to do this requires that one confront and surmount the defense mechanisms that one typically uses.

> Almost anything that extends our children's control over the world around them is bound to have a strong lure for them. In itself, that urge is a tremendous motivation for creativity and invention, for learning how to control disease or for finding ways to make deserts bloom.
> —Fred Rogers

Concluding Remarks

Throughout this book, we have stressed concepts that are not as prominent as they should be in business schools and courses in human and organization behavior. In stressing the human side of organizations, we realize that at times we have been unduly critical of ST. This is not because we do not value it. Indeed, Ian has his PhD in engineering, a field that is highly ST.

If we have been critical of ST, it is only because business schools generally neglect and even put down SF and NF, often in the harshest of terms. For instance, they insult it by calling it touchy-feely. We wouldn't insult a child by calling his or her feelings touchy-feely, and in this way say that they are unimportant. So why then do we do it to adults? Do their feelings matter any less?

We hope that this book helps to correct this situation. If anything, we believe that the world desperately needs integration along every conceivable dimension.

CHAPTER 25

Concluding Topics

We briefly need to discuss two other important topics: Knowledge Systems and the Boy/Girl Codes. Both topics relate to Life Skills and reinforce its importance.

Knowledge Systems

The Myers-Briggs in particular is extremely helpful in understanding the kinds of knowledge required for different kinds of problems.

If one is dealing with well-structured, bounded, defined problems—essentially exercises—that have one right answer, then ST is appropriate. But if one is dealing with open-ended problems that are ill-defined and have potentially many right answers, then the basic problems have many different formulations to begin with. As a result, NT and NF are called for.

If the S side of one's personality is particularly strong, then knowledge—truth in general—is a set of facts that are gained primarily through the senses, that is, that and only that which can be directly seen, heard, touched, and/or smelled. If one is an IS, then it is only what is gained through one's own senses that really matters. On the other hand, if one is an ES, then it is the shared sense impressions of experts that count; the more, the better.

If the T side of one's personality is dominant, then knowledge—truth in general—is a well-proven set of theorems like geometry, or a set of logical propositions.

If one is an NT, knowledge is in a whole system; that is, it is not a single set of facts or theorems (or theories), but a whole system of facts and theories.

For NFs, truth is often that which is the product of a good community debate.

If one is an integrator, knowledge is the result of the combined interplay between ST, NT, NF, and SF. That is, too much is riding on the solution to complex problems to base the definition and/or solution on any single way of looking at the world.

Every one of the fables we have encountered is about Systems Thinking, and unfortunately, most are about the lack of it. Indeed, Systems Thinking is at the heart of many of the Life Skills. It is certainly at the heart of making connections, critical thinking, and perspective-taking just to mention three of them. In this regard, King Friday is not a Systems Thinker. He is mainly trapped in his own perspective of the world and doesn't take others into consideration as in "The Bass Violin Festival" or "No Bare Hands in This Land." The King is also not systemic in making connections and being proactive about the mounting garbage problem and its effects on the total kingdom and the environment. But the same is unfortunately true of many of the other characters as well. They often do not consider the perspective of others and the total situation. That is, they do make important connections, both personal (NF) and impersonal (NT).

Of all the fables, Systems Thinking plays the major, dominant role in Planet Purple. Planet Purple is an old type, repressive organization, but as such, it is an old-line fragmented organization. For instance, feeling F and thinking T are considered to be entirely unrelated and therefore separable. In contrast, Planet Prism is a Systems Age organization. Everything affects everything else. Therefore, as much as is humanly possible, everything must be taken into account. That is, making connections is paramount.

No wonder why the shift between these two kinds of organizations is so profound and challenging. No wonder why critical thinking, communicating, and making connections—all of The Essential Life Skills—are essential in the jobs in the new, global economy.

A Basic Gap in Human Development

We need to address a basic gap in human development. Even though organizations are not responsible for the gap, the healthier an organization is, the more that it is aware of it, and the more that it tries to do everything in its power to overcome and to compensate for it, the more that it can deal with it. This is the good news.

Unfortunately, most organizations are not aware of the gap. As a result, they unknowingly reinforce it, and by doing so, make things worse. This is the bad news.

The good news is that those born in the 1990s and after (the Millennial Generation) are significantly less sexist, racist, and homophobic than previous generations, and therefore are substantially less subject to the issues and problems described later in this chapter.

The Boy Code

At precisely the time when children, and especially boys, need the words and the wisdom of a nurturing mentor like Fred Rogers the most, nature plays a cruel joke. Human biology, one's parents, peers, and society in general conspire to turn the feelings of boys inward, if not off altogether. They turn children away from the very sources that are available to help them to develop emotional health.

Around the age of five or six, most children, both boys and girls, find Fred Rogers babyish and corny. Action games, cartoons, and peers become the sources to which they turn for further development. But something even more insidious and devastating occurs in the development of boys. Harvard psychologist William Pollack refers to it as the Boy Code.[1]

Around five or six, young boys deliberately learn to turn off and to bury their feelings. It is as though a giant emotional switch has been permanently flipped to "Off." Even worse, if boys don't learn how to switch off and to suppress their feelings, then this can be utterly devastating. They will be picked on and bullied relentlessly by other boys for being "sissies".

This situation is rendered all the more tragic because when they are first born, boy babies are actually more emotionally expressive than girls. But mothers and fathers instinctively suppress their emotional responses toward their boy babies so that they in turn learn to suppress theirs as well.

To be sure, the feelings of young boys don't vanish altogether. This is impossible. They merely go underground where they remain primitive and undeveloped. By itself, this helps to explain the relatively low levels of emotional development of most—not all—men and most—but again, not all—organizations.

Where Fred openly acknowledged the fears and the emotions of very young children, and hence encouraged them to express them so they can be dealt with in constructive ways, society sends a clear and strong message that while it is acceptable for girls to express and to talk about their emotions, it is not for boys.

As young boys develop into adolescents, late teens, and early adulthood, they carry this numbing of feelings with them, often for their entire lives. There is compelling evidence that nature at last comes to the rescue in later years when men actively seek to recapture and to redevelop their lost feelings.[2] Nonetheless, for many men throughout the vast body of their careers, and their lives in general, they remain deeply estranged and alienated from their feelings.

While individuals feel the greatest impact of the Boy Code, there is however another important impact that is not generally recognized or acknowledged. Because it is so pervasive in our society, the Boy Code has had a profound effect on organizations. And, in fact, to our knowledge, no one has made the connection between the Boy Code and how it affects organizations.

Many organizations have been designed, albeit unconsciously, to help men keep their feelings at bay. Instead of aiding emotional growth and development, many organizations keep them emotionally stunted. They do this by enacting strong and sharp barriers between different corporate functions, business units, products, services, and so on (shades of Planet Purple). All this, of course, is defended in the language of economic efficiency. But this only begs the question as to why we tolerate this notion of efficiency. By denying one's emotions, is one truly efficient? We don't believe so.

Organizations put people into relatively rigid boxes, different "silos" that don't communicate efficiently or effectively with one another. In this way, they wall off people and their messy emotions from one another. Recall Planet Purple!

The Girl Code

As girls develop into women, many of them develop feelings of low self-esteem and the fear of challenging men. But something just as ominous happens to them as it does to boys.

Too many young girls turn their greater sensitivities with regard to feelings and to human relationships into weapons for bullying and humiliating other girls.[3] In turn, those who are bullied are often so desperate for relationships of any kind and extremely fearful of losing them that they will accept extremely harmful relationships over none at all. The phenomenon is akin to women who stay in abusive marriages. Those who are bullied often subordinate their needs for authentic relationships to those of any kind, however harmful they are.

As more and more women rise to senior ranks, we must take into account if and how they were hurt as young girls. If we do not, then we will not make organizations work for women as well as they need to work for men. For this reason, men and women both need to understand the Boy and Girl Codes.

For these and many other reasons, Fred's principles cannot be simply applied to adults, let alone organizations, without substantial modification. For instance, one cannot confront directly the lack of emotional development of most men. To do so only drives them further into the Boy Code, the set of unwritten rules that governs the behavior of individual men and of largely-male-dominated organizations. Instead, other strategies need to be employed to kick-start, if not to restart, the emotional development of men.

Helping men to develop their feeling sides involves much more than getting them to enroll in short courses and programs for developing emotional IQ.[4] It means dealing with the fact that the Boy Code underlies much of our current theories of business, economics, and organizations. It also means helping women to become more assertive and to overcome the hurtful relationships that they have had with other women in the past. Until these ideas are understood, and even more importantly, acted on, we will not be able to develop healthy managers and healthy organizations. We will continue to put mental and physical walls between others and ourselves.

The Traditional Masculine Code

The suppression of emotions is an important part of the Boy Code, but it is not its whole. As a result, treating emotions alone or in isolation will not result in healthier people or organizations. According to the psychologist Ronald Levant,[5] the Boy Code or the traditional masculine code is composed of the following:

1. The inability to feel, to identify, and to express feelings.
2. Overindulgence in anger; that is, anger is one of the few emotions men are allowed to have.
3. The propensity to simultaneously depend on, distance from, and take advantage of female partners.
4. Chronic fear and secret shame of failing to measure up as a man.
5. Overinvestment in work.
6. The lack of awareness of—or disregard for—the health risks associated with conforming to the traditional masculine code.
7. Discomfort with interpersonal and sexual intimacy.
8. The overall lack of relationship skills that makes closeness to others unattainable.

To put it mildly, there is a lot of work to do to change the way we live and work.

Summary Figures

The following figures in Table 25.1 summarize very briefly some of the main personality features of the main characters.

Table 25.1 Main Personality Features of the Main Characters

PLANET PURPLE

Lady Elaine Farchilde:
ENT
Competitive/Avoider
Relatively balanced life skills
Projection

GOOD FRIENDS

Lady Aberlin:
ST/NT initially   SF/NF later
Perspective taking—initially low
Communicating—initially low

Daniel Tiger:
SF
Communicating—initially low
Critical thinking—initially low

NO BARE HANDS IN THIS LAND

King Friday:
ISTJ
Competitive

THE BASS VIOLIN FESTIVAL

King Friday:
ISTJ
Competitive
Subjects:
Critical thinking
Challenging
Creative

THE RELUCTANT RING BEARER

Daniel Tiger:
SF
Anxious
Communicating—initially low
Critical thinking—initially low

ONCE UPON EACH LOVELY DAY

King Friday:
ISTJ
Unfocused
Not connected
Low self control
High avoidance
Residents NMB:
Focus
Self control
Handyman Negri:
ESFJ/ENFJ

DANIEL TIGER AND THE SNOWSTORM

Lady Aberlin & Neighbor Aber:
Critical thinking
Perspective taking
Daniel:
ISF/INF
King Friday:
ISTJ
Avoidant

Exercises

A Note to the Course Instructor

The following series of exercises have been designed to help students better understand the special topics presented in Chapter 16 by experiencing them directly. They are exercises in experiential learning.

Most of the exercises are designed to be administered before the students read the topic sections. For this reason, we strongly recommend that you familiarize yourself with all of the exercises and conduct them at the appropriate points during the course. While the exercises that the students should take before they read about the topics are especially important, we strongly encourage you to familiarize yourself with all of the exercises and give them to the students as you work through Part III of the book.

Depending upon their interpretation, all of the exercises can be used in conjunction with all of the special topic areas discussed in Chapter 16. Ideally, each exercise is to be conducted immediately before the students read the explanatory text for each of the special topics. Thus, the exercise that deals with Life Skills would be conducted immediately before students are assigned to read about Life Skills, the exercise that deals with Conflict Styles would be conducted just before students are assigned to read about Conflict Styles, and so on.

Life Skills

Introductory exercise: to be implemented *before* the students read the Life Skills section.

(a) Ask the students to think about two different days at work—a good day and a bad day. Then ask the students to write down three words that describe each day.

(b) Write "Good Day" and "Bad Day" on a flip chart. Go around the room asking each person to contribute one of their words to each list. Alternate between "good day" words and "bad day" words.
(c) Examine the words with the students. The words typically fall into at least these categories: time pressures, relationship issues, certainties/uncertainties, success/failure, and pleasure/pain. Add other categories that emerge from the lists.
(d) Discuss the categories. Point out that the underlying theme of all the descriptors is that they refer to what researchers call the Executive Functions of the Brain. Executive Functions are used to manage our attention, emotions, and behavior so that we can

- Reflect
- Analyze
- Reason
- Plan

(e) Follow the discussion by assigning students to read the section on the Essential Life Skills in Chapter 17. Point out

Conflict Management Styles

Introductory exercise: to be implemented *before* the students read the Conflict Management Styles section.

Setting up the exercise:

(a) Have all students complete and score the Thomas-Kilmann Conflict Mode Instrument (TKI). Versions of the instrument can be found online.
(b) Use the results of the instrument to form groups putting all like together, for example, Accommodators together, Avoiders together, and so on. Do not explain the basis for the groupings until after the exercise is complete.
(c) Give each group a copy of the scenarios outlined below. Have each group discuss each scenario in turn and be prepared to share their group response with the entire class.
(d) After each group has shared, explain the basis for the groupings. Point out that putting like types together exaggerates the type and makes it more obvious. Knowing one's own style and recognizing the different styles in others makes it easier to manage the different styles. This also makes it easier to adjust one's personal inclination to better suit the situation at hand. Assign the students to read the section on Conflict Management Styles.

(e) Consider repeating the exercise after students have read the material. For the repeat activity, put the students into groups containing mixed conflict management styles. Encourage them to note and consider how differently the mixed groups respond to the exercises.
(f) Point out that in general, Avoiders treat every situation as one to avoid.

Conflict Scenarios (Distribute the Following to All of the Groups)

(1) You, your family, and friends are in a burning building. Your lives are in grave danger. Time is of the essence. If you don't get out immediately, you risk losing your life and that of everyone else. Everyone is shouting and has a different idea as to what to do. If you were in this situation, what is your gut response? That is, what would you do instinctively without thinking about it?
(2) You and your colleagues are faced with a situation where people disagree over what to do about a problem. However, the problem isn't really very important to anyone. If you were in this situation, what is your instinctive gut response?
(3) You and your colleagues are faced with a situation where people disagree over what to do about a problem. While the problem isn't very important to you, it is to your boss especially since he or she feels that he or she has the right solution. If you were in this situation, what is your instinctive response?
(4) You and your colleagues are faced with a situation where people disagree over what to do about a problem. Since the problem is of moderate importance, it is necessary to get everyone's buy-in. If you were in this situation, what is your instinctive response?
(5) You and your colleagues are faced with a situation where people disagree over what to do about a particular problem. Since the problem is very important, it is necessary to examine the problem carefully, take your time, and get everyone's buy-in. If you were in this situation, what is your instinctive response?

Defense Mechanisms

Introductory exercise: to be conducted *before* the students read the section on Defense Mechanisms.

(a) Copy and distribute the situations below to each student. Instruct the students to read each situation and make notes for each of them. After completing the assignment individually, have students form pairs to share their notes.
(b) Following work in pairs, have each pair report back to the entire class or group.
(c) Assign students to read the section on Defense Mechanisms

Situations:

(1) List as many examples or cases of denial that you have read about, seen, or witnessed where denial is loosely defined as situations where individual people, organizations, or institutions were completely unable to face painful but important truths. Why were they unable to face them? Are you aware of any times that you have been in denial? Why? Who pointed it out to you? What caused you to acknowledge painful truths?
(2) List as many cases of disavowal that you have read about, seen, or witnessed where people, organizations, or institutions were only partially able to face painful but important truths? For instance, they recognized an important crisis or threat, but they minimized it considerably even if they didn't deny it completely. Why were they only partially able to face the truth? Are you aware of any times that you used disavowal to minimize important crises or threats? Why? Who pointed it out to you? What caused you to acknowledge the full threat, truth, and so on?
(3) List as many cases of compartmentalization that you have read about, seen, or witnessed where people, organizations, or institutions were only partially able to face painful but important truths? For instance, they recognized parts of an important crisis, threat, or problem, but they weren't able to acknowledge or see the whole. Why were they not able to see or face the whole truth? Are you aware of any times that you used compartmentalization to minimize important crises or threats? Why? Who pointed it out to you? What caused you to acknowledge the full threat or truth?
(4) List as many cases of projection that you have read about, seen, or witnessed where people, organizations, or institutions blamed others for crises or threats. Why did they blame others? Are you aware of any times that you used projection to minimize your involvement with an important crisis or problem? Why? Who pointed this out

to you? What caused you to acknowledge that you blamed others instead of accepting responsibility?

(5) List as many cases of projective identification that you have read about, seen, or witnessed where people, organizations, or institutions not only were blamed but also accepted the blame of others for crises or threats. Ask yourself, why did the people or organizations involved accept the projections of others? Are you aware of any times that you accepted or owned the projections of others? Why? Who pointed this out to you? What caused you to acknowledge that you did this?

(6) List as many cases of intellectualization that you have read about, seen, or witnessed where people, organizations, or institutions used abstract thinking to distance themselves from a crisis? Are you aware of any times that you used intellectualization? Why? Who pointed this out to you? What caused you to acknowledge that you did this?

(7) List as many cases of splitting that you have read about, seen, witnessed, and experienced where people, organizations, or institutions split the world into "good versus bad guys" and then blamed all of their problems on the bad guys. Why did they split the world into good versus bad guys and then blame the bad guys? Are you aware of any times that you used splitting to minimize your involvement with an important crisis or problem? Why? Who pointed this out to you? What caused you to acknowledge that you blamed others instead of accepting responsibility?

Personality Styles and Types

Introductory exercise: to be implemented before the students read the Personality Styles and Types section.

(a) Have all students complete a version of one of the Myers-Briggs personality type instruments that are available online.
(b) Each student is to submit his or her summary Myers-Briggs score (for example, ISTP) to the instructor. Create small groups by putting like types together. That is, put all the STs in one group, all the NTs in another group, all the SFs in another group, and all the NFs in another group. Each group should have about six to eight people. If the groupings are much larger than six, then subdivide the groups further by using the E/I and P/J dimensions so that all the ISTPs are in one group, all the ENFJs are in another, and so on.

(c) Prepare packets for each group. The packets should contain the following: a current issue of a popular news-type magazine such as *TIME* or *Newsweek* (each group gets the same issue), a pair of scissors and scotch tape, and a large piece of cardboard or paper.

(d) Announce the group assignments and have students gather into their assigned groups. *Do not* explain the basis for the group assignments at this time. Distribute the packets. The assignment is as follows: each group is to discuss and come to a consensus on "Society's Most Important Problem." (The assignment is deliberately left vague and open-ended. The objective is to have each group come to its own, unique definition of what society's most important problem means to them and them alone. The instructor is not to give them any more clarity or information, because the instructor would then be inserting his or her own Myers-Briggs personality type into the exercise.) The groups are to use the magazines, scissors, and tape to build a collage of images, words, and so on to illustrate their version of society's most important problem. When they are through, they are to give the collage an identifying, summary name. They are also to list as many characteristics and properties of their groups' collage/problem as they can. When finished, they are to be prepared to present their group's collage to the rest of the class. The groups have 30–40 minutes to complete the assignment.

(e) Each group is allowed five or so minutes to present their collage to the class. During the presentations, make notes on a flip chart of key words, concepts, and ideas from each group.

(f) After all presentations are complete, open a general discussion of the exercise:

- What did people think and feel as they heard and saw the different presentations?
- How were the group interpretations of the assignment alike? How were they different?
- How do members of different groups feel about the issue identified by other groups as Society's Most Important Problem? How do the issues differ from group to group?
- Ask students to reflect on the process within their groups. Was it hard or easy for them to come to consensus on the issue, on the ways to illustrate their issue? How cohesive were the group dynamics?

(g) Lecture/Group Discussion: Give a brief overview of the personality types. Explain how groups were formed, for example, by putting like types together. Explain that putting like types together magnifies and intensifies their particular way of seeing the world. Since like types generally find it easy to agree, this helps each group zero in on what they choose as a common problem. It also magnifies the differences between the groups. Further, by giving each of them the same exercise and the same magazines, the groups project their internal psychological dispositions onto something external so that others can see personality differences. That is, the collages allow one to see internal states of mind and psychological dispositions that are virtually impossible to see otherwise. In general, each Myers-Briggs group picks a very different problem, but even when they pick what seems on the surface to be the same problem, they treat it very differently bringing out the essential differences between them. For example, consider poverty: STs treat poverty primarily as a problem in microeconomics. That is, they treat poverty as a well-defined, bounded problem that is independent of all other problems. In their view, the problem of poverty can be solved merely by using the right monetary incentives that will induce employers to hire people for society's currently existing jobs. The right monetary incentives are also needed to induce people to get the right training that will prepare them for today's jobs, not for the pie-in-the-sky jobs of the future. NTs treat poverty as a problem of creating new educational systems that are needed to prepare people for entirely new jobs, many of which don't yet exist. NTs also ask, "What can we learn from other complex and systemic problems such as pollution that might shed new on poverty?" NFs treat poverty as a horrific human problem that causes whole communities unbearable pain. As a result, NFs want to set up new community-based organizations to help people when they are down and out. They ask themselves, "Can community groups be set up that will care for and watch children when their parents are learning new skills?" and "What counseling can be given to the chronically poor?" SFs want to adopt a single impoverished person that they can help as if that person was a member of their own family. "Treat everyone as if he or she is a brother or sister" is their motto. It not only sums up their definition of the problem but also their solution as well.

Most of the time, the Myers-Briggs groups easily recognize the differences between their group and the others. STs and NTs are perceived as technical, cold, and impersonal given they generally don't focus on human feelings. Where STs take a highly focused and detailed approach, NTs are expansive and systemic. In contrast, NFs and SFs are seen as highly personal. Where SFs focus on one person, NFs focus on entire communities, if not the entire nation as a whole. Many NFs even focus on world poverty. But then, many NTs focus on the world economy as the real source of the problem.

It is important to note that the psychological function (type) Feeling F and emotion are not the same. All the types can be highly emotional in defending their way of looking at the world. For each of them, theirs is often the only way of looking at something. In contrast, Feeling F is way of reaching decisions based on personal likes and dislikes. It is also a way of feeling with and about people.

In important situations, one wouldn't hesitate and not think of bringing in a professional translator if two or more people are speaking very different languages, French and Chinese for example, especially if none of them are fluent in the other's language. But we rarely bring in a translator when everyone is speaking English even though the words mean very different things to different people. This is unfortunate indeed for the chances for miscommunication are even greater.

Additional Reading

Ackoff, Russell. *Re-Creating the Corporation, A Design of Organizations for the 21st Century.* New York: Oxford University Press, 1999.
Campbell, Joseph. *The Hero With a Thousand Faces: The Collected Works of Joseph Campbell.* Novato, CA: New World Library, 2005.
Collins, Mark, and Margaret Mary Kimmel. Eds. *Mister Rogers' Neighborhood: Children, Television, and Fred Rogers.* Pittsburgh, PA: University of Pittsburgh Press, 1996.
Drucker, P. F. *The Essential Drucker: In One Volume the Best of Sixty Years of Peter Drucker's Essential Writings on Management.* New York: HarperBusiness, 2001.
Fraley, Chris. "A Brief Overview of Adult Attachment Theory and Research," http://internal.psychology.illinois.edu/~rcfraley/attachment.htm, 2010.
Galinsky, Ellen. *Mind in the Making: The Seven Essential Life Skills Every Child Needs.* New York: HarperStudios, 2010.
Grossman, Klaus, Karin Grossman, and Everett Waters. Eds. *Attachment from Infancy to Adulthood: The Major Longitudinal Studies.* New York: Guilford, 2005.
Keirsey, David, and Marilyn Bates. *Please Understand Me: Character and Temperament Types.* Del Mar, CA: Prometheus Nemesis, 1984.
Mitroff, Ian I. *Smart Thinking for Crazy Times: The Art of Solving the Right Problems.* San Francisco: Berrett-Koehler Publishers, Inc., 1998.
Mitroff, Ian I. *Why Some Companies Emerge Stronger and Better From a Crisis.* New York: AMACOM, 2005.
Mitroff, Ian I., with Gus Anagnos. *Crisis Leadership: Planning for the Unthinkable.* New York: John Wiley, 2003.
Mitroff, Ian I., with C. Murat Alpaslan. *Swans, Swine, and Swindlers: Coping with the Growing Threat of Mega Crises and Mega Messes.* Palo Alto, CA: Stanford University Press, 2011.

Mitroff, Ian I., with Elizabeth Denton. *A Spiritual Audit of Corporate America: A Hard Look at Spirituality, Religion, and Values*. San Francisco: Jossey-Bass Publishers Inc., 1999.

Mitroff, Ian I., with Harold Linstone. *The Unbounded Mind*. New York: Oxford University Press, 1992.

Mitroff, Ian I., with Abraham Silvers. *Dirty Rotten Strategies: How We Trick Ourselves and Others into Solving the Wrong Problems Precisely*. Palo Alto, CA: Stanford University Press, 2009.

Pollack, William. *Real Boys: Rescuing Our Sons From the Myths of Boyhood*. New York: Henry Holden Company, 1998.

Rogers, Fred. *You Are Special, Words of Wisdom from America's Most Beloved Neighbor*. New York: Viking, 1994.

Rogers, Fred. *Dear Mister Rogers, Does It Ever Rain in Your Neighborhood?* New York: Penguin, 1996.

Rogers, Fred. *The Mister Rogers Parenting Book, Helping to Understand Your Young Child*. Philadelphia: Running Press, 2002.

Rogers, Fred, with Barry Head. *Mister Rogers' How Families Grow*. Pittsburgh, PA: Family Communications, 1993.

About the Authors

Donna D. Mitroff

Donna received her PhD in Education and a Master's in Special Education from the University of Pittsburgh. She is currently the President and Founder of the children's media consulting group, Mitroff & Associates. With nearly three decades of experience in the entertainment industry—including commercial broadcasting, cable, and public television—Donna brings extensive working knowledge of the day-to-day management and production of children's television to Mitroff & Associates.

Donna has served as President of Mediascope (a nonprofit entertainment industry), Senior Vice President at Fox Family Worldwide, and Vice President of WQED West. In her various roles, she was responsible for developing strategies for her department, establishing policies and practices, fund-raising, creating partnerships, and supervising staff. She has significant production credits and has won several awards. She has served as Executive Producer for "Rinko: The Best Bad Thing," "You Must Remember This," and "The Fixer Uppers." She was the Executive in Charge of Production for the National Geographic Specials and for "Conserving America." She spent several years as Development Manager for "Wonderworks Family Movies" on PBS. As a specialist in the Children's Television Act, Donna has helped networks such as The Hub and production companies such as Cookie Jar Entertainment, American Greetings, Studio B, Chorion, Cinar, and SD Entertainment create shows that meet the Act's requirements.

Donna has been a member of numerous advisory committees and children's programming juries such as the American Center for Children and Media, the Children's Television Advisory Committee for Univision, DIC Educational Advisory Committee, NHK's Japan Prize, and the HUMANITAS Prize. She currently serves on the Advisory Board for Hollywood, Health & Society at the USC Annenberg's Norman Lear Center.

Donna also conducts and facilitates seminars on children and media issues. She is a frequent presenter of papers at national conferences. She has served as an Adjunct Professor in the Annenberg School for Communication at USC, where she taught several courses in children's media.

Donna was elected for three terms to the Board of Governors of the Academy of Television Arts & Sciences where she represented the Children's Programming Peer Group. She currently serves as a founding member of the committee that oversees the Fred Rogers Memorial Scholarship. In 2004, Donna was recognized as an Honoree at the Girls, Inc. Celebration in Los Angeles for "bringing research on child development to bear in children's entertainment, ensuring a higher quality in media and in children's lives."

Ian I. Mitroff

Ian has spent his entire career using interdisciplinary approaches to find successful solutions to complex problems. He is an emeritus professor from the University of Southern California (USC), where he taught for 26 years. While at USC, he was the Harold Quinton Distinguished Professor of Business Policy in the Marshall School of Business; he also held a joint appointment in the Department of Journalism in the Annenberg School for Communication at USC, where he taught Crisis Management and served as Associate Director of the USC Center for Strategic Public Relations. Currently, he is an Adjunct Professor in the College of Environmental Design and a Senior Research Associate at the Center for Catastrophic Risk Management, Haas School of Business, all at the University of California, Berkeley.

In addition to teaching, Ian serves as the President of Mitroff Crisis Management, a consulting group that offers an integrated approach to Crisis Management. For more than 35 years, he has been sought out as an analyst and consultant on human-induced crises, including major incidents such as the Bhopal Gas Tragedy, Three Mile Island, the scandal in the Catholic Church, Enron, the war in Iraq, the oil spill in the Gulf, and most recently, the tragic devastation in Japan due to earthquakes and tsunamis. He is widely regarded as one of the "fathers" of the modern field of Crisis Management.

Ian is the author of several well-received books, including *A Spiritual Audit of Corporate America* (Jossey-Bass, 1999); *Crisis Leadership* (Wiley, 2003); *Why Some Companies Emerge Stronger and Better from a Crisis* (AMA-COM, 2005); and most recently with Abe Silvers, *Dirty Rotten Strategies: How We Trick Ourselves and Others into Solving the Wrong Problems Precisely*

(Stanford, 2009), and with Murat Alpaslan, *Swans, Swine, and Swindlers: Coping with the Growing Threat of Mega Crises and Mega Messes* (Stanford, 2011). All in all, he has published 27 books and over 300 papers, articles, and op-eds. This is his 28th book. He is currently working on numbers 29 and 30.

Ian has an Honorary PhD from the Faculty of Social Sciences, the University of Stockholm. He is the recipient of a Gold Medal from the UK Systems Society for his life-long contributions to systems thinking. He is a Fellow of the American Psychological Association, the American Association for the Advancement of Science, and the Academy of Management.

He has a BS in Engineering Physics and an MS in Structural Engineering from the University of California, Berkeley. His PhD is in Engineering Science (Industrial Engineering) and the Philosophy of Social Systems Science from the University of California, Berkeley.

Fred Rogers' Biography

"You rarely have time for everything you want in this life, so you need to make choices. And hopefully your choices can come from a deep sense of who you are."

Fred McFeely Rogers was born on March 20, 1928 in Latrobe, Pennsylvania, forty miles east of Pittsburgh. Rogers earned his bachelor's degree in music composition at Rollins College in Winter Park, Florida in 1951. Immediately upon graduation, he was hired by NBC television in New York as an assistant producer for The Voice of Firestone and later as floor director for The Lucky Strike Hit Parade, The Kate Smith Hour, and the NBC Opera Theatre. Rogers was married in 1952 to Joanne Byrd, a concert pianist and fellow Rollins graduate.

Educational Television

In November, 1953, at the request of WQED Pittsburgh, the nation's first community-sponsored educational television station, Rogers moved back to Pennsylvania. The station was not yet on the air, and Rogers was asked to develop the first program schedule. One of the first programs he produced was *The Children's Corner*. It was a daily, live, hour-long visit with music and puppets and host Josie Carey. Rogers served as puppeteer, composer, and organist. In 1955, *The Children's Corner* won the Sylvania Award for the best locally produced children's program in the country. It was on *The Children's Corner* that several regulars of today's *Mister Rogers' Neighborhood* made their first appearances—among them, Daniel Striped Tiger, X the Owl, King Friday XIII, Henrietta Pussycat, and Lady Elaine Fairchilde.

During off-duty hours, Rogers attended both the Pittsburgh Theological Seminary and the University of Pittsburgh's Graduate School of Child Development. He graduated from the Seminary and was ordained as a Presbyterian minister in 1963 with a charge to continue his work with children and families through the mass media. Later that year, Rogers was invited to create a program for the CBC program in Canada, which the head of children's programming there dubbed *Misterogers*. It was on this series that Rogers made his on-camera debut as the program's host. When he and his wife and two sons returned to Pittsburgh in 1966, he incorporated segments of the CBC into a new series, which was distributed by the Eastern Educational Network. This series was called *Mister Rogers' Neighborhood*. In 1968 it was made available for national distribution through the National Educational Television (NET), which later became Public Broadcasting Service (PBS).

Lifetime of Achievement

In 1968, Rogers was appointed Chairman of the Forum on Mass Media and Child Development of the White House Conference on Youth. Besides two George Foster Peabody Awards, Emmys, "Lifetime Achievement" Awards from the National Academy of Television Arts and Sciences and the TV Critics Association, Fred Rogers received every major award in television for which he is eligible and many others from special-interest groups in education, communications, and early childhood. In 1999, he was inducted into the Television Hall of Fame. His life and work have been the subject of feature articles in national publications, including LIFE, Reader's Digest, Parents, Esquire, Parade, and TV Guide. In 2002, President George W. Bush presented him with the Presidential Medal of Freedom, the nation's highest civilian honor, recognizing his contribution to the well-being of children and a career in public television that demonstrates the importance of kindness, compassion and learning. On January 1, 2003, in his last public appearance, Fred Rogers served as a Grand Marshal of the Tournament of Roses Parade, and tossed the coin for the Rose Bowl Game.

Beyond the Broadcast

Fred Rogers was the composer and lyricist of over 200 songs, the author of numerous books for children, including the *First Experience* series and the *Let's Talk About It* series, and the author of many books for adults, including the *Mister Rogers Playtime Book*, *You Are Special*, *The Giving Box*,

Mister Rogers Talks with Parents, and *Dear Mister Rogers: Does It Ever Rain In Your Neighborhood?*. His last book, *The Mister Rogers Parenting Book*, was praised by *Publishers Weekly* for the "qualities of warmth and attentiveness that translate very well into this brief yet thorough parenting guide."

Fred Rogers received more than forty honorary degrees from colleges and universities, including Yale University, Hobart and William Smith, Carnegie Mellon University, Boston University, Saint Vincent College, University of Pittsburgh, North Carolina State University, University of Connecticut, Dartmouth College, Waynesburg College, and his alma mater, Rollins College.

The Fred Rogers Company

Fred was chairman of Family Communications, Inc. the nonprofit company that he formed in 1971 to produce *Mister Rogers' Neighborhood* and that has since diversified into nonbroadcast materials that reflect the same philosophy and purpose: to encourage the healthy emotional growth of children and their families. *Mister Rogers' Neighborhood* is the longest-running program on public television. Today Family Communications, Inc. is called The Fred Rogers Company in honor of its founder.

Fred Rogers died on February 27, 2003 at his home in Pittsburgh, Pennsylvania. He is survived by his wife, Joanne Rogers, their two sons, and three grandsons.

© The Fred Rogers Company—2011—All Rights Reserved

Notes

Chapter 8

1. Fred Rogers, Barry Head and Jim Prokell, *Mister Rogers Talks with Parents* (New York: Barnes and Noble Books, 1994), 43.
2. Thomas L. Friedman and Michael Mandelbaum, *That Used to Be Us: How American Fell Behind in the world It Invented and How We Can Come Back* (New York: Farrar, Straus and Giroux, 2011), 84.

Chapter 9

1. William Pollack, *Real Boys: Rescuing Our Sons from the Myths of Boyhood* (New York: Henry Holden Company, 1998).

Chapter 10

1. Ian I. Mitroff with Elizabeth Denton, *A Spiritual Audit of Corporate America: A Hard Look at Spirituality, Religion, and Values* (San Francisco: Jossey-Bass Publishers Inc., 1999); see also Leonard L. Berry, *Discovering the Soul of Service: The Nine Drivers of Sustainable Business Success* (New York: The Free Press, 1999).
2. Ian I. Mitroff with Gus Anagnos, *Managing Crises Before They Happen: What Every Executive and Manager Needs to Know about Crisis Management* (New York: AMACOM, 2001).
3. Christine Pearson and Christine Porath, *The Cost of Bad Behavior: How Incivility Is Damaging Your Business and What to Do about It* (New York: Penguin, 2009).

Chapter 11

1. Russell Ackoff, *Re-Creating the Corporation, a Design of Organizations for the 21st Century* (New York: Oxford University Press, 1999), 12.

2. Ian I. Mitroff and Abraham Silvers, *Dirty Rotten Strategies: How We Trick Ourselves and Others into Solving the Wrong Problems Precisely* (Palo Alto, CA: Stanford University Press, 2009).

Chapter 12

1. Parker J. Palmer, *Healing the Heart of Democracy* (San Francisco: Jossey-Bass, 2011), 5.

Chapter 13

1. Ian I. Mitroff and Elizabeth Denton, A Spiritual Audit of Corporate America, Jossey-Bass Publishers, San Francisco, CA, 1999.
2. Ibid.
3. Daniel Goleman, *Emotional Intelligence: Why It Can Matter More Than I.Q.* (New York: Bantam, 1995).

Chapter 14

1. Thomas L. Freidman and Michael Mandelbaum, *That Used to Be Us: How American Fell Behind in the World It Invented and How We Can Come Back* (New York: Farrar, Straus and Giroux, 2011), 91.

Chapter 15

1. Harold J. Leavitt, *Top Down: Why Hierarchies Are Here to Stay and How to Manage Them More Effectively* (Cambridge, MA: Harvard Business School Press, 2004).
2. Chris Lowney, *Heroic Leadership: Best Practices from a 450-Year-Old Company That Changed the World* (Chicago: Loyola Press 2005), 15.

Chapter 16

1. Ellen Galinsky, *Mind in the Making: The Seven Essential Life Skills Every Child Needs* (New York: HarperStudio, 2010).
2. Barbara Bund, *The Outside-in Corporation* (New York: McGraw Hill, 2006, pp. 30–33).
3. For a general discussion of demonizing, especially in politics, see Tom De Lucca and John Buell, Liars! Cheaters! Evildoers!: *Demonization*

and the End of Civil Debate in American Politics (New York: New York University Press, 2005).
4. R.D. Hinshelwood, *Clinical Klein* (London, UK: Free Association Books, 1994).
5. Carl Jung, *Psychological Types* (Princeton: Princeton University Press, 1971).
6. Ian I. Mitroff, *Why Some Companies Emerge Stronger and Better From a Crisis* (New York: AMACOM, 2005).
7. Jeremy Holmes, *John Bowlby and Attachment Theory* (New York: Routledge, 1994).
8. Klaus Grossman, Karin Grossman, and Everett Waters, *Attachment Theory from Infancy to Adulthood, the Major Longitudinal Studies* (New York: The Guilford Press, 2005).
9. Christopher G. Bresnahan, "Attachment, Group Functioning and Leadership: An Empirical Study" (University of Southern California: unpublished dissertation, 2007).

Chapter 17

1. Rogers, Head, and Prokell, *Mister Rogers Talks with Parents*, 42.

Chapter 19

1. Mitroff, *Managing Crises*.

Chapter 22

1. Mitroff with Denton, *A Spiritual Audit*.
2. Goleman, *Emotional Intelligence*.

Chapter 25

1. William Pollack, *Real Boys*; see also Ronald F. Levant with Gini Kopecky, *Masculinity Reconstructed: Changing the Rules of Manhood at Work, in Relationships, and in Family Life* (New York: Dutton, 1995).
2. Allan B. Chinen, *Beyond the Hero: Classic Stories of Men in Search of Soul* (New York: Putnam, 1993).
3. Rachel Simmons, *Odd Girl Out: The Hidden Culture of Aggression in Girls* (New York: Harcourt, Inc., 2002).
4. Levant, *Masculinity Reconstructed*.
5. Ibid.

Bibliography

Ackoff, Russell. *Re-Creating the Corporation, A Design of Organizations for the 21st Century.* New York: Oxford University Press, 1999.

Berry, Leonad L. *Discovering the Soul of Service: The Nine Drivers of Sustainable Business Success.* New York: The Free Press, 1999.

Brantley, Ben. "A Semi-Star Torn Between Two Superstars." *New York Times,* April 30, 2010. http://theater.nytimes.com/2010/04/30/theater/reviews/30everyday.html?

Bresnahan, Christopher G. "Attachment, Group Functioning and Leadership: An Empirical Study." (unpublished dissertation). University of Southern California, 2007.

Bund, Barbara. *The Outside-In Corporation: How to Build a Customer Centric Organization for Breakthrough Business.* New York: McGraw-Hill, 2006.

Chinen, Allan B. *Beyond the Hero: Classic Stories of Men In Search of Soul.* New York: Putnam, 1993.

De Lucca, Tom, and John Buell. *Liars! Cheaters! Evildoers!: Demonization and the End of Civil Debate in American Politics.* New York: New York University Press, 2005.

Drucker, P. F. *The Essential Drucker: In One Volume the Best of Sixty Years of Peter Drucker's Essential Writings on Management.* New York: Harperbusiness, 2001.

Friedman, Thomas L., and Michael Mandelbaum. *That Used to Be Us: How American Fell Behind in the World It Invented and How We Can Come Back.* New York: Farrar, Straus and Giroux, 2011.

Galinsky, Ellen. *Mind in the Making: The Seven Essential Life Skills Every Child Needs.* New York: HarperStudio, 2010.

Goleman, Daniel. *Emotional Intelligence: Why It Can Matter More Than I.Q.* New York: Bantam, 1995.

Grossman, Klaus, and Karin Grossman, and Everett Waters. *Attachment Theory from Infancy to Adulthood, The Major Longitudinal Studies.* New York: The Guilford Press, 2005.

Hinshelwood, R.D. *Clincial Klein*. London, UK: Free Association Books, 1994.

Holmes, Jeremy. *John Bowlby and Attachment Theory*. New York: Routledge, 1994.

Jung, Carl. *Psychological Types*. Princeton: Princeton University Press, 1971.

Leavitt, Harold J. *Top Down: Why Hierarchies Are Here to Stay and How to Manage Them More Effectively*. Cambridge, MA: Harvard Business School Press, 2004.

Levant, Ronald F., with Gini Kopecky. *Masculinity Reconstructed: Changing the Rules of Manhood at Work, In Relationships, and in Family Life*. New York: Dutton, 1995.

Lowney, Chris. *Heroic Leadership: Best Practices from a 450-Year-Old Company That Changed the World*. Chicago: Loyola Press, 2005.

Mitroff, Ian I., and Abraham Silvers. *Dirty Rotten Strategies: How We Trick Ourselves and Others into Solving the Wrong Problems Precisely*. Palo Alto, CA: Stanford University Press, 2009.

Mitroff, Ian I., with Gus Anagnos. *Managing Crises Before They Happen: What Every Executive and Manager Needs to Know About Crisis Management*. New York: AMACOM, 2001.

Mitroff, Ian I., with Elizabeth Denton. *A Spiritual Audit of Corporate America: A Hard Look at Spirituality, Religion, and Values*. San Francisco: Jossey-Bass Publishers Inc., 1999.

Mitroff, Ian I., and Donna Mitroff. "Spirituality in Action: The Fred Rogers Way of Managing Through Lifelong Mentoring." *Journal of Management Spirituality and Religion*. Vol 3, Issues 1, 2. London: Routledge, 2006.

Mitroff, Ian I. *Why Some Companies Emerge Stronger and Better From a Crisis*. New York: AMACOM, 2005.

Palmer, Parker J. *Healing the Heart of Democracy*. San Francisco: Jossey-Bass, 2011.

Pearson, Christine, and Christine Porath. *The Cost of Bad Behavior: How Incivility Is Damaging Your Business and What to Do About It*. New York: Penguin, 2009.

Pollack, William. *Real Boys: Rescuing Our Sons from the Myths of Boyhood*. New York: Henry Holden Company, 1998.

Rogers, Fred, and Barry Head, and Jim Prokell. *Mister Rogers Talks With Parents*. New York: Barnes and Noble Books, 1994.

Simmons, Rachel. *Odd Girl Out: The Hidden Culture of Aggression in Girls*. New York: Harcourt, Inc., 2002.

Index

Ackoff, Russell, 67
active listening, 90, 165
Aesop's Fables, 17
Alger, Horatio, 74
Andersen, Hans Christian, 17
Attachment Theory, 96, 123, 125–8, 133

Bakula, 1
Bennis, Warren, 89
Benson, Betsy, 6
Bowlby, John, 125–6
Boy Code, 169–72
    see also Girl Code
BP, 47, 49, 124
Briggs, Katherine, 109
    see also Myers-Briggs Type Indicator
Bryant, Adam, 58
Bund, Barbara, 98
Burton, LeVar, 1

Campbell, Joseph, 72–3
CEOs
    Crisis Management Teams and, 124
    King Friday as stand-in for, 4, 8, 63–4, 149–51
    leadership and, 88
    Myers-Briggs types and, 144, 149–51, 158
    Planet Purple and, 48
    rules and, 59
civility, 60
    see also incivility
cognitive flexibility, 98–100
Columbia School of Medicine, 72
Columbine shootings, 57, 140
comedy, 74
communication, 31–2, 103, 106, 128, 135, 155, 170, 180
    fables as, 4, 6–7
    Fred Rogers on, 2, 31, 90, 99
    leadership and, 89–90
    as a Life Skill, 96, 99–100, 168
    Myers-Briggs and, 116, 137–9, 164–5
    trust and, 85
compartmentalization, 48, 106–7, 133–5, 176
community, 8–9, 39–41, 49–50, 65, 72–3, 79, 123, 128
    connectedness and, 3
    Fred Rogers on, 3
    of learners, 104, 149
community-based organizations, 179
concern, 2–3, 10, 23–5, 47, 62, 113, 116, 128, 143

Conflict Management Styles, 104–6
Conflict Styles, 125, 145, 153, 156, 173
connectedness, 2, 128
    adults' need for, 56–7, 83–5
    community and, 3, 39
    creativity and, 100
    disconnection and, 48, 54, 77–80, 135, 158
    feelings, and, 56–60, 84–5
    Fred Rogers on, 19, 39
    Life Skills and, 96, 100, 149, 168
    Myer's Briggs and, 135, 139–41, 158–62
    organizations and, 49, 58–60, 141, 168–70
    spirituality and, 77–80, 159
consciousness, 2, 33–6, 78, 128, 159
Container Store, The, 78–9
courage, 2–3, 37–8, 65, 128, 152
creativity
    childlike quality of, 65–7, 152
    connections and, 100
    fear and, 65, 84, 151, 162
    Fred Rogers on, 2, 4, 27, 64, 91
    Myers-Briggs and, 111–13, 151–2, 160
    organizations and, 68–9, 80, 85, 91, 160, 162
    play and, 2, 4, 27–9, 65–7
    power and, 91, 165
    problem solving and, 64–9, 84–5, 151–2, 162
    trust and, 85, 152
Crisis Management, 96, 122–5, 128, 147

critical thinking, 4, 96, 100–1, 104, 123, 131, 135, 139, 140, 143, 161, 168
curiosity, 101

Daly, Tyne, 1
Defense Mechanisms, 106–8, 124–5, 128, 156, 165, 175–6
denial, 106, 108, 123–4, 133–4, 158, 161, 176
Diamond, Adele, 100
discipline, 59–60, 144–5
    see also rules
drowning in cereal, 161
Drucker, Peter, 98

emotional health, 9, 51, 87–8, 1–663, 169
emotional intelligence, 55, 98, 113, 138, 171
emotions, *see* feelings
empathy, 88, 90, 165
enthusiasm, 80–1
error of the third kind (E3), 64, 67–8, 150–1
Essential Life Skills, 96–104, 135, 140, 149, 155, 165, 168, 173–4
executive functions, 97–8, 174
exercises:
    Capstone, 127–9
    Conflict Management Styles, 174–5
    Conflict Scenarios, 175
    Defense Mechanisms, 175–7
    Ideal Organization, 121, 132
    Kidney Machine Problem, 118–20
    Life Skills, 173–4

Personality Styles and Types, 177–80
Train Crossing Problem, 120–1, 137

fables, 17–18
see also Neighborhood of Make-Believe, stories and fables
fairy tales, 17
Families and Work Institute, 97
Family Communications, Inc. (FCI), 1, 5
feelings
Boy/Girl Code and, 169–71
conflict management and, 105
connectedness and, 56–60, 84–5
creativity and, 66
disconnection from, 54, 135, 159
fables and, 18, 21
Lady Aberlin as sensitive to, 11
Myers-Briggs and, 109, 112–27, 133–5, 138–9, 144–5, 163–6, 168
naming, 21, 55–6, 138
Rewind Your Mind and, 56, 139
spirituality and, 80
see also emotional health; emotional intelligence
Fischer, Kurt, 97
focus and self-control, 96–8, 157
Fred Rogers Company (FRC), 1
Freud, Sigmund, 106, 108–9, 124–5, 153
Friedman, Milton, 49–50
Friedman, Thomas L., 53, 85

Galinsky, Ellen, 97–102, 104
Girl Code, 171–2
see also Boy Code

Grimms' Fairy Tales, 17
Gunnar, Megan, 102

Hartman, David, 1
Heckman, James, 104
Hero with a Thousand Faces, The (Campbell), 72–3
Hewlett Packard, 100
hierarchies, 73, 87–8, 163
hostile attribution bias, 99

Ideal Organization (exercise), 121, 132
incivility, 13, 60–2, 146–7
inhibitory control, 98, 100

job satisfaction, 13
Johnson, Wayne C., 100
Johnson & Johnson (J&J), 122
journey, 72–4
Jung, Carl, 108–10, 116–17

Kidney Machine Problem, 118–20
Kiehl's, 79
Kilmann, Ralph H., 104
see also Thomas-Kilmann Conflict Mode Instrument (TKI)
Knowledge Systems, 167–8

Lansing, Andy, 58
leadership
five principles of, 88–91
Fred Rogers on, 88–91
Jesuit model of, 91–2
power and, 91
preservative, 53
principles of, 163–5
transformative, 52–3
Leavitt, Harold J., 87
Levant, Ronald, 172

Levy Restaurants, 58
Life Skills, *see* Essential Life Skills

management, preservative vs. transformative, 52–3
Mandelbaum, Michael, 53, 85
Marshmallow Test, 98, 157
masculine code, *see* Boy Code
Maslow, Abraham, 77, 158
Matisse, Henri, 66
metacognition, 100–1
Mind in the Making (Galinsky), 97
mindset theory, 102–3
Mitroff, Donna, 1–2, 57, 140
Mitroff, Ian, 2, 58, 79–80, 107, 122, 141, 166
monsters, 72–3, 75
Morse, Aaron, 79
Myers, Isabel Briggs, 109
    see also Myers-Briggs Type Indicator
Myers-Briggs Type Indicator
    CEOs and, 144, 149–51, 158
    communication and, 116, 137–9, 164–5
    connectedness and, 135, 139–41, 158–62
    creativity and, 111–13, 151–2, 160
    feelings and, 109, 112–27, 133–5, 138–9, 144–5, 163–6, 168
    four combined types, 115–17
    group problem formulation and, 117–18
    Ideal Organization and, 121–25
    Introvert/Extravert (I/E), 110–11, 117
    Kidney Machine Problem and, 118–120
    Perceiving/Judging (P/J), 114–15
    rules and, 144–5
    Sensing/Intuiting (S/N), 111–12
    Thinking/Feeling (T/F), 112–14
    Train Crossing Problem and, 120–21

needs hierarchy, Maslow's, 77, 158
Neighborhood of Make-Believe (NMB)
    characters in, 10–12
    overview of, 8–12
Neighborhood of Make-Believe, stories and fables
    "Bass Violin Festival, The" 4, 27–9, 35, 63–9, 149–53, 157, 168
    "Daniel Tiger and the Snowstorm," 37–8, 83–4, 161–2
    "Good Friends," 19–21, 55–6, 85, 137–8
    "No Bare Hands in This Land," 23–5, 59–60, 143–4, 168
    "Once Upon Each Lovely Day," 33–6, 77–8, 157–8
    "Reluctant Ring-Bearer, The," 31–2, 71, 90, 155–6, 164
    "Story of the Planet Purple, The," 39–41, 45–54, 71, 131–5, 168, 170–1

omnipotence, 2, 37, 90, 165
organizations
    community-based, 179
    fables and, 3, 18
    families as, 25
    hierarchies and, 73, 87–8, 163
    Ideal Organization (exercise), 121, 132

job satisfaction and, 13
methods for changing, 51–3
as neighborhoods, 14
Planet Prism vs. Planet Purple, 47–54, 56–60, 78, 87, 134–5, 139–41, 145, 163, 168
repressive organizations, 46, 133, 168
see also CEOs
Outside-in Corporation, The (Bund), 98

Palmer, Parker J., 76
Personality Styles and Types, 108–29, 132–5, 167, 172, 177–80
perspective-taking, 96, 98–9, 135–40, 143, 146, 168
Pittsburgh Magazine, 6
Planet Prism vs. Planet Purple organizations, 47–54, 56–61, 71, 78, 87, 134–5, 139–41, 145, 163, 168
play, 2, 4, 27–9, 65–7, 152
Pollack, William, 57, 169
preservative leadership, 53
preservative management, 53
projection, 107, 124, 132, 176–7
projective identification, 106–7, 177
Psychological Types (Jung), 109

quest, 73, 80, 159

rags to riches, 74
rebirth, 75
repression, 108
repressive organizations, 46, 133, 168
Rewind Your Mind, 56, 139

Rogers, Fred
on active listening, 2, 90
on change, 13
on children's control over their world, 91
on communication, 2, 31, 90, 99
on connection, 19, 39
on creativity, 2, 4, 27, 64, 91
on diversity, 50
on giving and receiving help, 3
inducted into the Academy of Television Arts and Sciences Hall of Fame, 1
influence on adults, 6–8
on the invisible part of ourselves, 2, 33
on kindness, 88
on leaders, 88
on loving what you do, 89
on ministry, 79
on omnipotence, 2, 37
Pittsburgh Magazine's legacy issue on, 6
on play, 2, 4, 27, 64, 90
as Presbyterian minister, 7, 79
on relationships, 2, 19
on rules, 2, 23, 62, 104
study of child psychology, 7
on transitions, 47, 134
on values, 36
Rogers, Joanne Byrd, 1
Rudeness, *see* incivility
rules
importance of, 2, 23–5, 59–62, 97, 143–4, 153
Myers-Briggs types and, 144–7
Planet Purple and, 40–1, 46
see also Conflict Styles

Schultz, Howard, 71
self-directed learning, 103–4

self-discovery, 88–9, 164
Seven Cs, 2–3
   see also communication; community; concern; connectedness; consciousness; courage; creativity
sexual harassment, 60, 145
solving the wrong problem precisely, 64, 67–8, 150
songs
   "There Are Many Ways To Say I Love You," 20–1
   "You Can Never Go Down the Drain" (song), 5
Southwest Airlines (SWA), 14, 58, 141
spirituality, 7, 67, 77–81, 158–9
splitting, 106–7, 124, 177
Starbucks, 71
stories and storytelling, 72–55
   see also Neighborhood of Make-Believe, stories and fables
Sweeney, Anne, 6

technology, 63–5, 68, 78, 83, 89, 112, 120, 150–1, 159, 162
That Used To Be Us (Friedman and Mandelbaum), 53, 85
Thomas, Kenneth W., 104
Thomas-Kilmann Conflict Mode Instrument (TKI), 104–5, 174
Tomlin, Lily, 1
Top Down (Leavitt), 87
"Tortoise and the Hare, The" (fable), 17
tragedy, 74–5, 121
Train Crossing Problem, 120–1, 137
transformative leadership, 52–3
transformative management, 52–3
"Tribute to Fred Rogers, A," 1–2, 6

voyage, 72–4

working memory, 98, 100
World War II, 125
WQED (public television station, Pittsburgh, PA), 1

Zappos Shoes, 58, 141
zero tolerance policies, 60–1, 145–6

CPSIA information can be obtained
at www.ICGtesting.com
Printed in the USA
BVHW04*0848060418
512674BV00006B/10/P